SAFARI

SAFARI

BARBARA RADCLIFFE ROGERS
Principal Photography by GERRY ELLIS
and STILLMAN ROGERS

CRESCENT BOOKS

NEW YORK

A FRIEDMAN GROUP BOOK

This 1991 edition published by Crescent Books, distributed by Outlet Book Company, Inc.,
a Random House Company, 225 Park Avenue South, New York, New York 10003.

ISBN 0-517-69341-0

SAFARI
was prepared and produced by Michael Friedman Publishing Group, Inc.
15 West 26th Street, New York, New York 10010

Editor: Elizabeth Viscott Sullivan
Art Director: Jeff Batzli
Designer: Kevin Ullrich
Photography Editor: Christopher C. Bain

Typeset by M&M Typographers, Inc.
Color separations by Excel Graphics Arts Company.
Printed and bound in Italy by Eurograph spa

8 7 6 5 4 3 2 1

DEDICATION

To Julie and Lura—neither of them knows Africa yet, but they will one day come to love it as I do, Lura for its animals and wild places, and Julie for its varied peoples and their rich cultures.

SOME WORDS OF THANKS

In the years of travel that preceded this book and made it possible, the lists of friends, hosts, rangers, and outfitters have grown long. A few of them deserve to be mentioned for their special contributions.

Closest to the bush itself, and thus most influential in setting fire to my imagination, are the rangers and guides with whom I have traveled many long, rough miles of Africa. Most notable among these for their knowledge and love of the bush are Jonathan Swart and Neil Outram. Each has played a major role in making this book possible.

The hospitality and genuine interest of camp owners and managers is one of the hallmarks of a good safari, whether in a rustic fly camp or a polished, permanent lodge. Suzanne and Tony Bignaut, owners of Inyati in the Sabie-Sand Reserves have always extended their hospitality, even when the camp was closed. My appreciation also to Tony Williams of Harry's Huts—as fine an out-doorsman as he is a camp manager; to Shelagh Aikman of A World Apart; to Brigitte Ramruth and Cecil Bartlett of Pom Pom Camp; Clare and Bruce Cantle of Machaba; and Shareen and Richard Nash of Shindi Island, whose camps are superlative outposts of civilization, comfort, and com-radery in the vast wilderness of the Okavango Delta.

Any good safari is taken with good traveling companions and mine have been the best. From the bleary-eyed moments of daybreak to the fireside conversations late into the night, I have been blessed with good company in my African travels: Sara Godwin, Leslie Simpson, Annie Moller, Jerry and Suzanne Schottke, Eva Schmid, Wolfgang Wegner, Toby Constantine, and Charlie Pinkney. And Tim, for sheer endurance and good humor as we moved together on safaris through five countries, as good company at breakfast in the bush as he is at dinner in Johannesburg.

A special thanks goes to friends made along the way, whose help, encouragement, and hospitality are the things that keep travelers going: Barbara Jeppe of Johannesburg, Bettie Wessels of Pretoria, Phyl Palmer of Maun, Jane and Clive Froom, and Don Smith of Nairobi.

Perhaps the next three names should have been first, since each was involved in a major way with the very beginnings of the ventures on these pages. Peter Celliers first introduced me to the beauties of the eastern Transvaal—my first taste of the African bush and still my favorite corner of it. With

Peter began not only this book, but what has become a compelling drive to see as much of Africa as a lifetime will permit.

My friend Dick Griffiths introduced me to the man who would take charge of my travels and fortunes over the course of several safaris: Mark Hamilton of Classic Tours International in Chicago. Mark did for me no more and no less than he does for all his clients, but he did it so well that, safari after safari, every detail fell into perfect place. It was he who suggested A World Apart and Flamingo Tours in Nairobi and Ker Downey Selby in Botswana. His advice on where to go, what to see, how long to stay, and even what to eat and drink, was golden. I could not have trusted my travels to better hands.

Because it is so far away, Africa is not a place to visit on week-long trips. Mine have ranged from two weeks to well over a month in length, growing longer with each successive venture. This has only been possible because life goes on at home and office under the competent management of my mother, Dee Radcliffe, and my daughter, Julie. Neither of them has seen Africa, but it is only through their understanding and help that I have been able to. To them, and to my younger daughter Lura, who has grown up explaining "I'll have to wait until my mother gets back from Africa," my biggest thanks of all.

CONTENTS

© Gerry Ellis/Ellis Wildlife Collection

INTRODUCTION

*S*afari! No single word thrills the soul of a traveler quite like the simple Swahili word for *journey*. Little did the East Africans know, in the days before the "great white hunters" and their bearers moved across the land, that this one word would grow into a symbol of a new kind of travel, and, for many, into a symbol of Africa itself. To today's travelers, a safari is a journey into the remote reaches of an untamed or unexplored land, a journey in search of exotic wild animals.

The white hunters are gone, and their bearers laden with campaign chests live only in faded photographs and old etchings. But the call of the African bush is more alive than ever. To those who have never smelled the clean African morning or felt the sting of its afternoon dust in their eyes, it is a place of dreams. For those who have, it is a place of memories, a raw world whose landscapes haunt us like no others on earth.

Some say it is the unique smells of the bush that make the African landscape so compelling—the combination of pollens and oils from the continent's myriad plant species that fills the air. Others

Opposite page: *The hagenia forests of Rwanda, while filled with their own wildlife, are not a common safari destination because of their remote location and impenetrable nature.*

© Lee Kuhn/FPG International

Opposite page: *The yellow acacia, known locally as fever tree, is only one variety of the many acacias of the African bush.*

Left: *Browsers, such as giraffes, can easily share a habitat with grazing animals like zebra.*

point to Africa's extraordinary colors, soft and harsh, dramatic and subtle all at once. The reds and yellows of the sands, the rich blue of the skies, the deep black-green of the ebony trees, the gray of the thorn, the jagged blacks of tree snags, the russet of the bush willow, the silver of morning sun on the reed plumes, the slight haze of dust that softens everything.

Primal and vital, the world of Africa's wildlands brings everyone who sees it face to face with themselves and their origins. The twentieth century meets the dawn of mankind and the brutal essence of the wild here, and the contrasts are at times overwhelming.

It is not just the wild animals that fascinate and excite people on safari; it is the land itself, the trees and grasses teeming with life, the flowers, the mountains in sharp escarpments, and the dramatic cones of volcanos.

Environments range from bushveld to rain forest, from desert to the web of rivers and streams in a vast delta. In between there are the thirstlands, dry riverbeds, rock kopjes, plateaus, rushing torrents, thundering waterfalls, open woodlands, dense forests.

No place stirs the senses quite like Africa. The rich variety of her landscapes, and her many cultures and peoples create a combination of exotic and gracious, wild and highly civilized environments. It is an exquisite combination, and if you let it, it will invade your memory with its sensuous patterns and rhythms and never let go of you.

THE HISTORY OF SAFARIS

When we think of the safaris of old, in the tradition of the European explorers and white hunters, it is East Africa—the Kenya, Tanzania and Uganda of today—that come to mind. But expeditions to East Africa were by no means the first. For many years, hunting and naturalist expeditions explored only southern Africa—today's Botswana, Zimbabwe, Namibia, and Republic of South Africa. Only much later did East Africa become the hunter's Eden.

To understand the reason for this we must look to the maps of the world as it was in the 1800s and consider where the explorers and hunters were coming from. In the dawning years of the nineteenth century, most settlements on the African continent were trade and supply stations along the African coast that had served the East India trade since the Dutch first settled Cape Town in 1652.

The British took over the Cape colony in 1806 and abolished slavery there. The Dutch farmers, angered at the loss of their "property," began their long move north. They went with their families and their livestock, their wagons laden with supplies, with the purpose of establishing farms. It was

Opposite page: Members of the Livingstone expedition fire into an oncoming herd of Cape buffalo.

15

"To wander through a fairy-land of sport among a new and fabled creation amid scenes never before paced by civilized foot is so truly spirit-stirring and romantic, that in spite of hardships the witchcraft of the desert must prove irresistible."

Cornwallis Harris: **The Wild Sports of Southern Africa,** *1838*

Opposite page: *Long lines of bearers were needed to carry the trophies collected on hunting expeditions.*

these "voortrekkers," later known as the Boers, who settled the inland areas of the Transvaal.

The first white travelers to go into the bush were an assorted lot. There were the missionaries bent upon "Christianizing the heathen," the traders intent upon business, the ivory hunters out to make their fortunes on elephant tusks—and there were the explorers. Among the explorers were the naturalists, astonished by the enormous variety of previously unknown flora and fauna, and anxious to collect specimens of all of them. Nearly all the explorers came from England. Ambitious colonizers like Cecil Rhodes pushed the boundaries of British rule further and further into the interior of the continent, until the British Empire was spreading so fast that London could hardly keep up with the responsibility of governing it.

East Africa remained an Arabic stronghold, with trading stations and slave markets run from the East coast. To get there, Europeans had to make the long trip around the Cape and up the entire East coast of Africa. Cape Town was a much closer starting point for inland expeditions, and was under British control. Even the British hunter Frederick Selous, whose name is still inextricably linked with East Africa, began his career with years of exploration in southern Africa.

William Burchell, formerly a gardener at the Royal Gardens at Kew and an ardent botanist, arrived in Cape Town from Britain in 1810. Delighted with the hundreds of plant specimens that he discovered in the Cape Peninsula alone, he resolved to explore further into the interior than any other botanist had previously gone.

His journey was to be the forerunner of the great safaris to follow, safaris that would crisscross much of the African continent. More than half a century before the word safari would be used to denote this kind of adventure, William Burchell mounted an expedition that would inspire and instruct all that came after him.

Burchell's journey began with six months of preparation: He built a sturdy wagon to withstand the mountains, rivers, and long treks across the veld; hired Africans to accompany him; and put in supplies. Since he was going into unexplored land, he had to anticipate every need. Firearms, gunpowder, tools, medical and art supplies, and an abundance of items to trade for services and safe passage filled the wagon, which was pulled by a team of oxen.

He traveled for four years, recording and drawing his botanic specimens, as well as much else he encountered—including the Tswana language, since he was the first European to venture into the

land of the Bechuana. His observations went far beyond his botanical training, covering geology, anthropology, zoology, and even astronomy. He collected 40,000 specimens, discovered several new animal species, and wrote volumes of diaries. The specimens that Burchell took back to England with him, his engravings, and his published diaries fascinated his fellow Englishmen and inspired some of them to follow him.

The next great safari was mounted by an avid hunter who had studied Burchell thoroughly. Cornwallis Harris was a sportsman, and his venture in 1836 into the vast interior of southern Africa in pursuit of game was the first hunting safari. The trek of the Boers into the Transvaal was well under way by this time, with settlements established farther north than in Burchell's time.

Crossing the vast desolate areas of salt pan and stone, Harris came to the game-rich lands of the Tswana. Also a painter, Harris made detailed and zoologically accurate drawings and measurements of every animal he encountered. He told in his diaries of springbok by the millions covering the veld, but even in those days lamented the disappearance of other game due to over-hunting. He also wrote of the plight of the Bushmen, driven to even more barren and inhospitable lands, hunted down by the Boers and other local tribes alike.

His route went deep into the northern Transvaal, east of Burchell's, and over the Limpopo River into present-day Zimbabwe. He marveled at the beauty of the Magaliesberg Mountains, where he finally found elephants. Harris was the first to record his observations of the sable antelope and decided at that point to return to England. After only five months out he went back to his homeland claiming to have two perfect heads of every known game animal in southern Africa.

Harris's sketches and animal observations were highly perceptive, and he also compared what he saw to Asian species. He published a book, *Wild Sports of Southern Africa*—and a collection of his engravings of animals, which in turn excited a new generation of young Englishmen to follow him. Since his was the first hunting safari, it became the standard for others to follow. Problems were never as difficult as when he encountered them, yet a century later, hunters were still reading his book before they set out.

Gordon Cummings developed his interests and skills in the wild by hunting in northern Scotland. Resigning his commission after serving in India and the Cape Colony, Cummings set out on a safari longer than Burchell's by more than a year. He covered much of the Transvaal and Bechuanaland,

FPG International

now Botswana, in search of game that had by 1844 been forced farther north by the encroaching Boer farmers.

An early safari pauses at the foot of Mt. Kilimanjaro.

Still using an ox-drawn wagon, Cummings too returned with enough ivory to finance his expedition, but he hunted and kept his journals with little of the naturalist spirit that guided his predecessors. He admired the game and felt deeply moved by their beauty and majesty, but he was a hunter. Back in England in 1850, with his collection of literally tons of trophies and artifacts, he lectured widely and wrote *The Lion Hunter in Southern Africa*, adding to the enticing literature of the safari.

Unlike others who had come to Africa dreaming of a safari, David Livingstone was already there. As a missionary and avowed enemy of the slave trade, he lived with his wife, Mary, in what is now

Dr. David Livingstone was among the lucky few who lived to describe the experience of being attacked by a lion.

Botswana. Although he never lost his Christian zeal, Livingstone's writings show his ever-increasing interest in geographical exploration and in the wildlife that still filled the area.

Accompanied by William Cotton Oswell, Livingstone explored the Kalahari Desert in search of Lake Ngami. Oswell was a hunter with a taste for exploration, and he had the money that Livingstone lacked. They shared an abhorrence for slavery and an understanding of the land and the peoples that they traveled among. It was Oswell who taught Livingstone the art of bush survival.

Both men were fascinated by the local tribesmen's tales of the Lake Ngami, which was the subject of many myths, and is to this day a great enigma. The lake survives on the overflow from the Okavango Delta, and geological evidence shows that it was once about 1,016 square miles (1,800 sq km) in size. By the time Livingstone and Oswell saw Ngami in 1849, it was only about 75 miles (120 km) in diameter; it has diminished even further in the past century to a bare 155 square miles (250 sq km) at its fullest.

Although not originally a hunter, Livingstone became quite an expert at game hunting during the course of his travels across Africa from the Atlantic to the Indian Ocean (though he was once badly injured by a lion during a hunt). At that time, it was necessary for every safari to shoot enough to feed itself.

After their discovery of Lake Ngami and exploration of the edges of the Okavango Delta, Livingstone and Oswell made the first safari to the Zambezi River, reaching a point less than 100 miles (160 km) from Victoria Falls, which Livingstone would discover on a later trip. It was the first trip which inspired Livingstone to make his subsequent four-year journey across Africa.

The cross-continent journey, even more than his earlier safaris, illustrates Livingstone's unusual qualities as a missionary. Evangelizing was not his prime concern, although he indoctrinated entire tribes into Christianity. He was far more interested, particularly in his later years, in putting an end to slavery and mapping the unknown reaches of the continent.

Cotton Oswell left a legacy of his own, as well as what he added to the safari tradition in the company of Dr. Livingstone. He was a sportsman's sportsman; to him hunting was a gentlemanly sport with its own code of fair play. Like many hunters that came after him in Africa, he was aware of the need for conservation. He treated the tribal peoples with respect and in turn earned theirs. He was a generous guest in their land, occasionally staying and hunting for a hungry village until it was well fed.

Drawn to Africa by Gordon Cummings's book, William Charles Baldwin arrived shortly after Oswell returned to England. With neither personal fortune nor wealthy comrades to back him, Baldwin earned his way through the bush, shooting for meat and selling ivory and skins to support his safaris across the Kalahari and through much of what is now Botswana, Zimbabwe, and Zambia. Because his were not luxury safaris, his diary records ten years of bush experience with more attention to practicalities than those of explorers who came before him.

To many, the greatest Africa hand of all was Frederick Selous. As a boy, he read the diaries and books of the great hunters and sharpened the skills he would later need in the wild. Oswell and Livingstone were his heroes. In 1871, at age nineteen, he sailed from England for southern Africa. Gold

Frederick Selous, one of the first professional "white hunters," was a close friend of President Theodore Roosevelt. Selous planned the president's expedition to Africa to collect museum specimens.

and diamonds had brought settlement to the Transvaal, and both the game and the native inhabitants had retreated into the north. Selous followed them across the Limpopo.

Like Baldwin's, Selous's safari was sparsely equipped. Selous depended heavily on his own skills, traveling without horses and hunting elephant on foot. He and his small party lived off the land. He was a keen observer and learned the habits of the game he hunted. He also respected the experience of his Bushman companions, learning from their hunting and survival skills.

Selous became the prototype for Allan Quatermain in Rider Haggard's novel *King Solomon's Mines*. After eight years in Africa, Selous published his own book about his adventures. Within a few years he was guiding other English hunters on safari, which began a trend. Guided safaris and invention of the breach-loading rifle made big game hunting easier, and African journeys more accessible to the sportsman-traveler.

Cecil Rhodes, in an effort to secure further lands, asked Selous to lead a group of settlers into the area south of the portion of the Zambezi River that forms part of the present Mozambique border. Rhodes hoped that establishing outposts there would discourage Portuguese slaving raids in the region. The route taken on this expedition, known as the Selous Road, was later lined with a series of forts.

Selous continued to write—as much of natural history as of his adventures—and although he returned to England to live, he made many more hunting trips to Africa and elsewhere. His detailed drawing and descriptions became the standard reference for East African animals.

Up until the end of the nineteenth century, most safaris were made by the English. But Selous's close friendship with President Theodore Roosevelt began the American interest in safaris. Fired by the stories Selous told to the Roosevelt children in the White House, the president asked Selous to help him plan his own African hunting safari. It was Selous who anticipated the rise of East Africa as a safari destination. The Roosevelt safari was to inaugurate not only this area, but the coming wave of American game hunting in Africa.

With the opening of the Suez canal, East Africa became easier for Europeans to reach. Kenya was close to the Suez, and the British quickly recognized its importance as a base from which to control the coastal area. This was vital if they were to keep the Suez Canal open as a trade route to India. By that time, the Victorian British were also bent on putting an end to slavery by the Arabs and among the African chiefs themselves, who offered slaves to traders in exchange for goods. Kenya was a major slave route for Arab traders, and a base there was essential if this commerce was to be stopped so that British colonial influence could expand.

East Africa offered many natural advantages to safari travelers. The habitats were rich in diversity, and in the days before air travel, they were easier to reach from coastal ports than the wilderness of southern Africa, which still required long overland journeys.

Perhaps the first man to envision the possible future for Kenya was Lord Delamere. He came to Kenya a reckless spendthrift at age twenty-one, having succeeded to a barony at seventeen. He took part in several early, ill-fated hunting adventures, but he kept coming back despite sunstroke, typhoid, riding accidents, and being mauled by a lion, which left him with a permanent limp.

In 1896 he outfitted an expedition into Somaliland to explore one of Africa's few remaining uncharted regions. Returning without injury for once, he was determined to settle in East Africa and chose a spot near Nakuru to build Equator Ranch. Here, also, he was beset by problems, but he managed to overcome them. He was, above all, persistent and resourceful. He tried everything, from innkeeping to meatpacking. He was endlessly active in the political, social, and economic life of Kenya, and is credited more than anyone else with the success of the colony.

Delamere was one of the first to realize that hunting, game conservation, and human development had to be carefully balanced if Kenya were to survive. It was his idea to combine the Masai lands with game preserves, since the habits of the one did not interfere with the needs of the other.

His farm became a stopping point for important visitors on safari. He had made all his farms into game sanctuaries, and his guests hunted the predators and others that threatened the balance between crops and wildlife. There were other colonials who "came out" to hunt and stayed to farm, but Lord Delamere was the larger-than-life prototype for all of them. His name is nearly inseparable from that of colonial Kenya.

Nairobi continued to grow, both as a staging point for the increasing number of safaris, and as home base for the rising number of settlers in the colony. As Nairobi began to take on the veneer of European civilization that the British brought with them wherever they settled, so did safaris. Although farming and commerce were the mainstay of the colonials, the safari was becoming their lifeblood.

Cecil Rhodes expanded British settlement into what is now Zimbabwe and Zambia in an effort to stop the Portuguese slave trade.

North Wind Picture Archives

FPG International

Opposite page: *"Big tuskers" like this one were once a highly prized trophy for any hunter.*

Left: *Rhinos, although never as plentiful as elephants, were one of the first animals whose numbers were depleted by hunters.*

Farmers doubled as professional white hunters, the guides who took hunting parties out on safari. The custom of hiring a European guide as an escort and aide-de-camp that had begun long before in the early sporting safaris of the southern colonies of Rhodesia and Bechuanaland (now Zimbabwe and Botswana), and in South Africa was continued here by Selous.

Nairobi grew from a small settlement to the safari capital of the world, the staging point for a new kind of hunter who came for a holiday. These hunters did not want to spend several months mounting an expedition, hiring a staff and guides, purchasing wagons and laying in provisions. Their needs begat the outfitter, local hunters who made all of these arrangements and had the safari ready to go when the client arrived.

An experienced hunter, Theodore Roosevelt took an active part in planning his safari, relying heavily on the advice of his old friend Frederick Selous. Roosevelt's was not a holiday safari but, the trip of a lifetime for the man who, more than anyone else of his day, was responsible for the protection and preservation of wilderness areas and wildlife both in the United States and abroad. Sponsored by the Smithsonian Institution and the American Museum of Natural History in New York, for which he would collect specimens, the safari included three professional naturalists.

FPG International

The safari of Kermit and Theodore Roosevelt was not only covered closely by the American press, but encouraged other Americans to follow in their footsteps.

Opposite page: *Today's tented safaris still use tents much like those employed on the Roosevelt safari.*

When the president alighted from the Mombasa train, three hundred people who would be a part of the expedition as bearers, porters, and camp staff were waiting. On the trail, the party stretched nearly a mile (1.6 km) in length.

Theodore Roosevelt and his son, Kermit, traveled and hunted in four countries with the best hunters of their day—Selous, Lord Delamere, Sir Alfred Pease, and their expedition manager, R. J. Cuninghame. Along with the game, Roosevelt took great interest in the birdlife of Kenya's lakes and delighted in the land itself. He relished camp life, often hunting until dark and returning by moonlight to the campfire.

As for colonial Kenya, the Roosevelt expedition was a blessing well worth the hospitality lavished on this first celebrity safari. Associated Press followed him with its own safari and sent daily bulletins home. These, and Roosevelt's own dispatches and articles, were eagerly read by a generation of Americans with the resources to follow him.

In the years following the turn of the century, before World War I turned East Africa into a battleground, the hunting safari flourished. Each boat that docked in Mombasa brought more hunters or collectors from zoos and museums. As cameras became more portable, photographers joined the hunters.

For many of these people money was no object, and soon luxurious Nairobi clubs opened to accommodate wealthy safari clients. Full-course dinners of wild game were served on china, and champagne and brandy from crystal glasses, a tradition that lives on in luxury safaris today.

Into this prewar Kenya came more legendary hunters, settlers and travelers, all adding their own style and flair to the safari world. Dennys Finch Hatton arrived and established a farm just before the outbreak of the war.

Safaris stopped while everyone defended the British colonies from the German forces. The hunters, already skilled in the bush and handy with weapons, joined with the Masai to patrol borders. Delamere, Finch Hatton, and even Selous, who had long since retired to England, joined forces to protect Kenya. Selous was killed by a German sniper while on duty with his regiment, made up of seasoned Africa hands from England. He is buried in the remote game preserve in Tanzania that still bears his name.

After the war, the safari business boomed again, in what many consider to be its golden age. More

farmers, like Bror Blixen, left their plantations for others to manage and took to the bush as professional white hunters.

Supplies were now carried by motor vehicle, and clients often moved by plane. Camps were comfortable, even luxurious, with service that included stand-up tents with beds, hot showers and iced drinks. The wines were as good as the fireside conversation. Today's classic tented safaris are based on this period.

One of the most unusual and perhaps most fascinating characters in this halcyon safari world was Beryl Markham, daughter of an unsuccessful English farmer. She was raised in the bush with Nandi boys, learning hunting and survival skills from them and horsemanship from her father. As a fearless bush pilot, she became part of the safari world, often in the company of Blixen and Finch Hatton. Markham, like Bror Blixen's wife, Karen (Isak Dinesen), wrote of her experiences in Kenya, documenting Kenya's safari heyday in a literature all its own.

The first major photographic safari lasted for four years and was mounted by Osa and Martin Johnson in 1924. Toting the cumbersome motion picture equipment of the day, the Johnsons traveled to a little-known volcanic lake in northern Kenya. This environment was home to enough birds, animals, and flora to keep their cameras busy for their entire stay.

Not strictly a safari, in the sense of moving camp constantly from place to place, the Johnsons' expedition established a permanent base at Lake Paradise, and built log cottages to live in and a darkroom. From there they made frequent long safaris in search of different wildlife and environments.

Dennys Finch Hatton became one of the first professional hunters to publicly encourage photographic safaris and condemn the growing practice of hunting from automobiles. He advocated a blend of photography and sportsmanlike hunting, which would keep the industry busy and clients happy, and also stop the drain on the game population.

When the Prince of Wales, later King Edward VIII, came to Kenya, it was just such a safari that Finch Hatton took him on. The future king was a good shot with both camera and rifle. He returned to England with trophies of both kinds, but became a strong advocate of the photographic safari.

The prince's safari may have marked the beginning of the era of the photographer in the bush, but hunting safaris continued in Kenya until they were banned in 1977. Game had decreased at an

Most pictures like these make the sport of hunting appear to be that of a lone man against an elephant; they do not, however, reveal the number of armed attendants usually standing behind the hunter.

FPG International

alarming rate from both hunting and poaching, threatening the future of tourism and the country's wild heritage.

Decades earlier, South Africa and Zimbabwe instituted strong antipoaching measures. They launched programs to protect the survivors of their herds that were so successful that regular culling was necessary to protect their habitats. Hunting safaris continue in these countries now but are strictly controlled. Enormous licensing fees provide revenue for game conservation research and an efficient means of keeping populations in balance.

Although there has been an attempt to redefine the word *safari* to mean only a hunting trip, the word is far broader in scope, both historically and in its Swahili usage. *Safari's* origins are in the Arabic verb "to discover." Its use today, covering excursions in search of wild animals or environments—be they armed with a camera, or simply with interest—is in the fullest sense correct.

The photographic safari is now the backbone of the industry throughout the game areas of Africa. Although styles vary greatly among different outfitters, much of the charm and style of earlier days still live in the classic safari. Some safaris are little more than bus tours from hotel to hotel, but there are several outfitters specializing in customized adventures that have a lot in common with hunting safaris of the past. Often led by men whose bush wisdom was gained as white hunters, the emphasis is on the experience, not on simply covering territory or bagging great numbers of animals, either on film or on a checklist.

These safaris are designed for those who relish the sounds and smells of the bush and want to be a part of its rhythms. But the thrill of the hunt is still there, especially in safaris on private land or reserves that allow foot or off-track travel.

Although four-wheel-drive vehicles have replaced the ox cart and T-shirts have replaced beads as a tourist's best medium of trade, today's traveler can have much of the experience of the early hunter, tracking game on foot through the bush or in an open cruiser with nothing between the hunter's camera and the lion walking calmly toward it.

The great safari still lives in the areas where it began—Botswana and the Transvaal—and in Kenya and Tanzania, where it later flourished and made its name. And it will continue as long as there is wild game in Africa and people who long to watch the stately giraffe or the lumbering elephant move in its own wild world.

Opposite page: Not as sought after for trophies as other animals, antelopes such as this lesser kudu were hunted as meat to feed those on safari.

MODES OF SAFARI

Each traveler has his own vision of the ideal safari. For some it's days of pounding over the dusty plains in a hatch-roofed or open truck, pitching camp at the end of the day and cooking dinner over a camp stove. For those who prefer things less rugged, a real safari might begin with the take-off of a tiny bush plane from Nairobi or Maun, headed to a small tented campsite, all set up and waiting beside a river or lagoon.

For others, a safari means staying in a series of modern lodges set high on rock kopjes above the Serengeti Plain or on the rim of an ancient crater. Still others dream of safari evenings spent in comfort in the aura of one of Africa's colonial farms or coffee plantations, or seated, drink in hand, high above a floodlit water hole where the wildlife will come to them.

Birders will envision a lodge set in the bird-rich shoreland of Lake Naivasha, or a camp amongst the rookeries of the Okavango. Those who feel seeing game is more important than travel might choose a lodge in a game-rich area such as the Sabie-Sand Reserves.

Opposite page: *Balloon safaris, popular in the Masai Mara, have stirred controversy among game authorities since they are thought to disturb the wildlife more than the game-viewing vehicles do.*

Permanent tented camps, such as this Ker Downey Selby camp at Machaba in the Okavango Delta, are very much like the movable camps of the classic safaris.

THE TENTED SAFARI

Exclusive tented safaris, custom-designed to suit the interests and needs of a private group, are closest to the classic tradition of the early Africa travelers. These safaris can go almost anywhere—from the floor of the Ngorongoro Crater, where game drives take up the early morning and evening hours, before and after visitors staying in the rim lodges are allowed into the crater, to the remote and beautiful Loldaiga Hills, where the day might begin with a two-hour game walk with no other visitors to mar the quiet.

These private camps are set up for a single party of guests. It may be one couple, a family group of eight or ten, or a group of friends who enjoy traveling together. Groups are never combined, even if two couples want exactly the same itinerary at the same time.

The tents on this kind of safari are room-size, with twin beds, plenty of walking space, and hand-woven rugs on the floor. They have verandas, dressing rooms, and attached washtents as well.

Meals are meticulously planned and prepared, and elegantly served outdoors or in a dining tent. As in any bush camp worthy of the name, there is fresh-baked bread every day.

Camp days are as full or as restful as guests choose. For the intrepid there are trails to explore, birds and flowers to photograph, and animals to track through the low woods and high grass. There is a water hole to watch and the cool shade of the tent's awning in the afternoon for reading or catching up on your day log or wildlife notes.

After a few days in one place, guests on these exclusive safaris usually spend a night or two at a lodge, such as The Ark or Treetops near Mt. Kenya, or at a colonial farmhouse, while the camp is packed up and moved to the next destination. When all is ready and the champagne is chilled, guests are flown by bush plane to the new campsite.

At the other end of the luxury scale, but every bit as real in terms of the experience of living in the bush, are the group safaris where everyone pitches in. Facilities vary greatly, from large tents with cots to sleep-on-the-ground fly camps under mosquito netting. Everyone is a participant rather than simply a guest, pitching and breaking camp, cooking meals, doing laundry, loading, unloading, and sharing other camp tasks.

Instead of going on a morning game drive or hike and coming back to a hot breakfast, group members do the cooking and wash the dishes themselves. This camp offers a comradery and sense of participation that many travelers enjoy.

Since the groups on these organized tours are assembled at random, they are a good way for solo travelers to meet others and enjoy a group experience. Also, without the staff of fifteen that luxury safaris carry, and without the multicourse meals, these are in a much lower budget range.

Tented safaris, whatever their style, are an unparalleled chance to experience the bush at its best. As long as reasonable precautions are taken—keeping tent entrances closed at night, not wandering around alone after dark—living in the bush is quite safe. Travelers on these safaris will see and learn about far more than the large animals they came to see; they will learn why the whistling thorn whistles and how to distinguish the calls of the evening birds from the chirp of a fruit bat or reed frog.

© Stillman Rogers

"*Nothing but breathing the air of Africa, and actually walking through it, can communicate the indescribable sensations which every traveller of feeling will experience.*"

William Burchell: **Travels in the Interior of Southern Africa,** *1824*

A World Apart is one of the few safari outfitters allowed to pitch camp in the yellow acacia grove on the floor of the Ngorongoro Crater.

Right: *At Tarangire Safari Lodge in Tanzania, tents are protected by thatched-roof bandas.*

Opposite page: *A hagenia forest in Rwanda.*

SAFARI CAMPS

Instead of moving a camp from place to place, setting up the tents, and building temporary kitchens each time, safari camps are set up permanently in one place. Tents are room-size, but instead of attached washtents they have permanent bathrooms in reed enclosures. The tents are very often set up under open thatched bandas and like the luxury movable camps, they have hot showers.

Dining room and lounge areas are permanent structures, usually open at the front, overlooking a river, water hole or lagoon. With a campfire in front to welcome guests back from their afternoon game drive, they provide a casual gathering place.

The camp routine is much like that of the private safari, with game drives and walks tailored to the interests of guests. The capacity of these camps varies, but it is usually around twenty. Unless one large party has reserved the entire camp, there will be a variety of guests, who will be divided into groups for game drives. At dinner, everyone is seated at one or more large tables, so there is a lot of opportunity to meet and socialize with other travelers.

THE CAMP KITCHEN

Whether prepared at a permanent camp or a movable one, safari food can be equal to that of a fine lodge with all the modern conveniences. The camp kitchen runs on a minimal amount of electricity—usually just enough to run the refrigeration units. To preserve the quiet of the bush, the generators are normally not operated while the guests are in camp.

Cooking is done over wood fires. In permanent camps, these are usually in stone or cement fireplaces set inside a reed kitchen enclosure open to the sky. In a bush kitchen, fires are built in the open and pots are set directly on the fire or on small portable grates. Food is prepared out of doors, in the shade of a canvas awning or in a covered area inside a kitchen enclosure. Despite the primitive cooking facilities, varied and sophisticated dishes can be served at every meal, each properly chilled or piping hot.

Nearly every camp bakes fresh bread daily in a metal oven. These heavy boxes are set into a pit in which a fire has been burning. Hot coals from the fire are left under the box and more from the cooking fire are shoveled on top to provide an even heat. Although controlling the temperature of this oven is even more tricky than controlling a woodstove, crisp, delicious loaves of hot bread seem to appear effortlessly.

At Shindi Island Camp in the Okavango Delta, the chef has mastered the use of the tin oven to the point where souffles are a regular feature of his menus. The only mishap he's had with this tricky dish in his unpredictable oven is an occasional overbrowned top, which is easily removed just before the soufflé is served.

Each camp manager has his or her own style of cooking. Brigitte Ramruth at Pom Pom missed her fresh herb supply and planted a garden in the corner of her kitchen enclosure. From the hard-packed delta silt she harvests parsley, basil, thyme, and chives for the lively and innovative cuisine that has made Pom Pom a favorite stop in the Okavango.

Brai, or grilled meats, are a dinner classic throughout the camps of southern Africa. At least one dinner in Botswana or the eastern Transvaal will feature this traditional mixed grill, which always includes some wild game. Especially in the Transvaal, herds of impala and some other types of animals multiply at such a rate that they must be culled regularly, so the venison is served to guests at the lodges and camps.

Benson, the Tswana cook at Shindi Island Camp in the Okavango Delta, cooks all the meals in, over, or under open fires—with results that any restaurant would be proud to serve.

© Stillman Rogers

© Stillman Rogers

A World Apart bakes fresh bread daily in tin ovens buried under the fire.

Chobe Game Lodge, shown here, is set in gardens along the banks of the Chobe River.

SAFARI LODGES

Usually located in parks or private reserves rich in game concentrations, lodges may be hotels or more like resorts, with individual suites or bungalows. Those located on private land, such as the lodges of the Sabie-Sand Reserves, offer a full schedule of game drives and walks. Guests usually stay at these for several days, enjoying the relaxing atmosphere and fine foods as well as the opportunity to see a wide variety of game and habitat with well-trained and enthusiastic rangers. Accommodations are luxury class, often in thatched cottages set in lush tropical gardens. Meals are served in a dining room, on the verandas, or in a *boma*, a round reed enclosure open to the sky and with a campfire in the center. This is often used for grilling dinner as well.

Lodges in the public parks such as the Serengeti tend to be more like hotels. Although they serve three meals a day, and some people do stay longer than one night, their programs do not include game drives or other activities. Most game viewing is done with privately hired drivers during the travel between lodges.

Parks such as the Kruger, in the eastern Transvaal, offer rest camps. These have both self-catered bungalows and rondavels without cooking facilities, where travelers can stay between days of driving their own cars through the park to view game. Some of these have campgrounds as well, for people who carry their own tents and gear.

"Still watching" is another way of viewing game, and some lodges are set up for this special purpose. Instead of taking guests to the game, these lodges bring the game to the guests. This method, developed in the 1930s and refined to an art by Eric Sherbrooke-Walker, involves a lodge built above a natural water hole. Block salt is placed near the water as a further attraction to the animals. Sherbrooke-Walker's original Treetops lodge was literally a treehouse in the forest that was later to become Aberdare National Park in Kenya.

Especially successful in forest habitats where travel is difficult and visibility limited, this type of game viewing also provides a good chance to see nocturnal animals. Still watching has also been adopted by several more traditional camps, such as Mashatu, in the Tuli Bloc in southern Botswana. The dining room and lounge areas there overlook a well-lighted riverbank almost directly below, where guests enjoying their evening drinks can watch animals coming for theirs.

Although still watching rarely appeals to the adventurous as a substitute for being in the bush, a night or two in one of these lodges is very enjoyable and can add another dimension to a safari.

Guests at Tarangire National Park can sit on the terrace in front of the main lodge and watch elephants and other wildlife that come to the river to drink.

MODES OF TRAVEL

The ways of getting from camp to camp are as varied as the accommodations. As mentioned earlier, on a luxury tented safari, guests are flown or driven from one camp to the next, usually staying three or four nights, with a stop at a lodge or private farm in between, while the camp is being relocated. These safaris are more common in Kenya, where there are several parks and reserves separated by fairly long distances. Fly-in safaris are the most common means of travel in the Okavango Delta as well, where overland travel is difficult and distances also great.

In areas such as the Masai Mara and Serengeti, the path between lodges leads through vast park areas, where one of the delights of travel is the chance of finding a pride of lions beside the road or a herd of giraffes munching the tops of the thorn trees. Although the days are long and often hot and dusty, animals and birds in these parks are so plentiful and varied that this is the best way to see them.

Right: *Large vans with open-roof hatches are used for road travel and game viewing.*

Opposite page: *The crowned crane is one of the showier of the many bird species common to East Africa.*

© Gerry Ellis/Ellis Wildlife Collection

© Stiliman Rogers

Open vehicles, such as this one at Machaba Camp in the Okavango Delta, offer the best game viewing and photography, as well as the ability to travel into off-road areas where vans cannot go.

© Stillman Rogers

Although the old dug-out log mokoros are more romantic, they leak badly, so Pom Pom Camp has replaced them with modern metal boats of the same shape.

Those who are looking for a really unique safari can even travel between camps in northern Kenya by camelback. Great fun in their own right, and a good way to see an entirely different environment, these safaris are not done in regions with great animal concentrations, so they are not a good choice for game viewing.

In the Okavango Delta, travel on safari is often by power launch or dugout canoe called a *mokoro*. These craft are poled through the shallow waterways where there are no channels for larger craft. In northern Botswana, "Sundowner" cruises on the Chobe River offer the chance to view animals from the water as they come in the evening to drink.

Game-viewing vehicles vary greatly as well. In the Ngorongoro Crater and other rough terrains, a four-wheel-drive jeep or truck is required. These usually do not have open roofs. For long days of

riding, most travelers are more comfortable in small vans that have pop-up roof hatches. These offer quick, unobscured visibility, and welcome protection from the equatorial sun without wind and dust in the face. The condition of Tanzania's roads make travel by van considerably more comfortable than the rougher ride of a four-wheel-drive truck.

In the Sabie-Sand, at both the Rattray Reserves and Inyati, game viewing is done from open jeep-like vehicles. Since drives are in the early morning, late afternoon, and evening, exposure to the sun is not a problem. The open tops and sides of these vehicles give visitors more of the look and feel of the bush. Similar, but higher, open vehicles are used by several camps in the Okavango Delta. The added height is welcome there, not only for seeing over the tall reeds, but for safety and comfort when the road disappears into a watercourse several feet deep.

Overcrowding in many of East Africa's larger parks has caused many safari-goers to choose lesser-known parks where there is more plentiful game and fewer visitors.

EXPEDITION GEOGRAPHY AND WILDLIFE

The popular view of an African safari through vast jungle-covered areas is an inaccurate one. Actually, there is very little jungle in the parts of Africa where there are wildlife concentrations. Eastern and southern Africa, where the great game reserves and parks are located, are varied in their terrain, but in general are open and arid with only seasonal rains.

The predominant landscape is veld and vast savannah, cut by riverine valleys and rock outcrops (kopjes). In Tanzania the face of this terrain occasionally rises into a volcanic mountain, such as Kilimanjaro or an ancient collapsed crater, such as Ngorongoro. In Kenya the skyline may be dominated by the jagged lines of the Aberdares' summits or craggy, snow-capped Mt. Kenya.

Cutting through the best of the wildlife regions of both countries is the Great Rift Valley, an ancient geologic crack in the earth, its wide floor and slopes now filled with fertile soil and covered with farms and plantations. In the lower parts of the valley are found the strange soda lakes which form from highly alkaline waters caused by leeching from the volcanic slopes that surround them.

Opposite page: *Although the vegetation in the area between the Ngorongoro Crater and the Serengeti National Park may seem too sparse to support large animals, the giraffes find good browsing in the tender acacia tips.*

51

Pages 52-53: Mt. Kilimanjaro provides a backdrop for game viewing in Kenya's Amboseli National Park.

In South Africa the majestic Drakensberg escarpment rises in a dramatic wall above the bushveld; between Zambia and Zimbabwe the Zambezi River drops off the face of a sheer cliff into a deep, narrow crack in the earth's surface where it is then confined to create a rushing, frothing torrent. In Botswana's Okavango Delta, almost endless waterways meander through a vast flat land, bringing green to its landscape year-round.

These geographic features, each a dramatic variation from the land around it, provide contrast to the otherwise similar landscapes. A lazy river full of hippos disappears suddenly over a several-hundred-foot cliff. The vast brown Kalahari desert gives way suddenly to the bright green and blue of papyrus-filled lagoons. A flat, barren landscape of dust and sparse grass hummocks drops into a flat and fertile valley floor. A narrow road winds precariously along the rim of a caldera, with the Rift Valley visible straight down on one side and the Ngorongoro Crater 2,000 feet (700 m) below on the other. An outcrop of giant rounded boulders and cliffs breaks through the flat surface of the Serengeti Plain. Just as you begin to think that you know what the land looks like, it becomes entirely different.

At first glance, the vast areas of veld, savannah, and thornbush between these great geologic wonders may seem monotonous—horizon to horizon of brown in the dry season. But as you move across them, they take on a character all their own. Seen up close, each becomes a habitat, and after a day or so, the safarigoer realizes that any bush could have a lion within its cool shade, every thorn grove a herd of elegant giraffes nibbling at the tops. The next tall tree could well have a leopard asleep on an overhanging limb. Or a pack of rare wild dogs may appear suddenly out of the grass on the side of the road. The cloud of dust at the horizon may be a huge dark tide of wildebeests, the advance garde of a massive annual migration.

Getting to know the habitats and the life they support is half the fun of a safari. It is a proud day when the traveler can spot a pride of lions before the tracker or ranger sees it, or point the way to a kill by watching the increasing circle of vultures wheeling about somewhere in the sky.

African habitats can generally be classified as savannah, desert or thirstland, forest, and wetland. Within each of these are a number of variations.

Savannahs are dry landscapes, usually grass covered, which may have scattered trees or thornbush on them. They may give way to open forests with little or no undergrowth, or they may be covered in low growth, such as the mopane "forests" of southern Botswana. Grazing animals—the gazelles, antelopes, wildebeests, and zebras—are common in these areas where grass is plentiful, and browsers such as giraffes will be found in the savannah where there are enough trees and shrubs to provide them with food. Wherever there are grazers and browsers the carnivores will also be found. Lions, wild dogs, cheetahs, leopards, and hyenas are all in the savannah, as are jackals, vultures, and other scavengers.

The Masai Mara, Serengeti, and eastern Transvaal are the best known and most accessible savannah destinations, but there are a number of others with excellent game concentrations: Chobe and the Tuli Bloc in Botswana, Samburu and Tsavo in Kenya, and Ngorongoro and Tarangire in Tanzania, to name a few.

Forest areas are more densely wooded, often with underbrush as well as trees. Browsers, such as bushbucks, are at home here, along with primates and tree-climbing predators such as the leopard. Elephants move between the forests and the savannah, but are much easier to spot in the savannah, where their legs do not masquerade as tree trunks and their bodies cannot hide behind dense foliage. The Aberdare and Mt. Kenya areas of Kenya and Mt. Kilimanjaro in Tanzania offer excellent forest habitats, as does the Rwanda volcano where the mountain gorilla is found.

Wetlands include swamps, ponds, rivers, lakes, and lagoons, as well as much of the Okavango Delta. Since rivers and lakes are found in savannahs, these small wetlands offer good views of savannah animals that go there to drink. Wetlands provide habitat for hippos and crocodiles, as well as the enormous variety of birds that live on the fish, insects, and fruit-bearing plants that thrive in these areas.

The Okavango Delta in Botswana is southern Africa's outstanding wetland. The four great lakes of Kenya's Rift Valley—Baringo, Bogoria, Nakuru, and Naivasha—along with Tanzania's Lake Manyara, are East Africa's major wetlands.

Deserts are dry regions, some of which spring very briefly into bloom or grass cover during the rainy season. These—the Kalahari of Botswana, Namibia, and South Africa included—are really thirstlands and not true deserts. They support many of the same grazers that live on the savannah; migration habits of these animals are much more pronounced as they follow the seasonal water supplies. The carnivores then follow these grazers.

The reticulated giraffe is easily distinguished from the common giraffe by its clearly defined pattern of reddish spots.

Page 56-57: The waterbuck is found throughout most of the safari regions of Africa, where it feeds on varieties of grasses that other grazing animals don't eat.

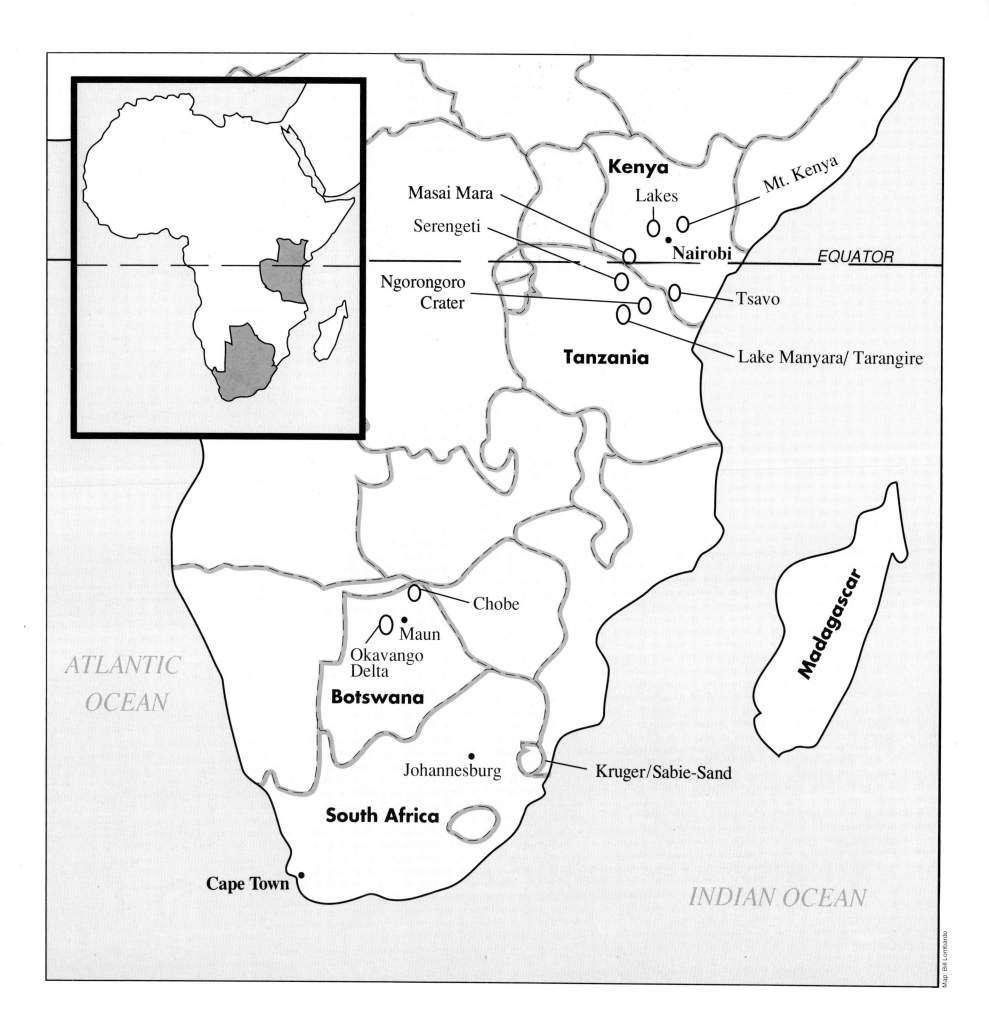

THE FACE OF AFRICA

Each of the primary game-viewing areas of Africa offers its own unique landscape, habitats, wildlife, and styles of safari. These combine in an almost infinite variety, and there are no two areas that could be called the same. The safari experience in each of these places is governed by its location, terrain, and the history of travel there, as well as by the politics and economy of the country and its peoples' attitudes toward wildlife. Within these variables, each visitor finds something different, and brings on safari a personal knowledge or interest that colors the experience.

Some regions may offer a wide variety of safari options, while others may have only one or two. In Botswana's Okavango Delta, for example, nearly all safaris are of the fly-in variety because of the difficulty of overland travel in the swamps.

The variety of safari experiences and game-viewing areas is as wide as the face of Africa itself.

THE MT. KENYA PARKS

Clustered around the base of Mt. Kenya are some of Africa's best-known lodges and best small parks for game viewing. Lying just barely north of the equator, the area's climate is made temperate by its elevation and by the cooling breezes that come off the mountain slopes.

The exception to this is Samburu Reserve, somewhat north of the others, which is hot and dry. It is a classic example of arid habitat, a semidesert region of scattered scrub vegetation at a 3,000 foot (914 m) altitude. Only the Ewaso Ngiro River provides a year-round water source, and it is here that the game eventually gathers into concentrations that make good game viewing.

Elephants are the main attraction, along with a few rhinos that have escaped the poachers. Hippos, reticulated giraffes, leopards, cheetahs, lions, gerenuk, Grévy's zebras, oryx, and other denizens of arid habitats are easy to spot in this barren environment. The animals are not as plentiful as in the Serengeti or the Sabie-Sand, but Samburu offers good game viewing nonetheless.

© Gerry Ellis/Ellis Wildlife Collection

Opposite page: *Elephants are gregarious animals, and one often found in large herds.*

Left: *The forests of northern Kenya are home to Hartlaub's turaco, commonly called the lourie.*

"Through the bright sunlight we saw in front of us the high rock peaks on Kenia [sic], and shining among them the fields of everlasting snow which feed her glaciers: for beautiful, lofty Kenia is one of the glacier-bearing mountains of the Equator."

Theodore Roosevelt: **African Game Trails,** *1910*

Although it lies at the equator, Mt. Kenya has a permanent ice cap at its summit.

There is a luxury lodge on the river bank and a permanent tented camp. Another way to see Samburu is with your own safari, camped along the river a good distance from these structures, where the great, vast, dry land meets the water under a grove of giant acacia trees.

Higher in altitude and closer to the base of Mt. Kenya, Meru National Park offers a wide variety of habitats and a cool climate. It lies along the Tana River at the point where the dry plains meet the grassy savannah and the wooded slopes of Mt. Kenya's foothills, and is cut by streams and swamps where it is not uncommon to see herds of more than one hundred buffalo. Zebras fill the plains, followed by lions and an occasional cheetah or leopard. Hundreds of bird species live in this region, making it a favorite addition to the birding circuit of the lakes to the west.

An interesting feature of Meru is the herd of white rhinoceroses introduced here from South Africa. This rhino has become extinct everywhere except in the Natal, where it has long been carefully protected. As a result, the South African herd increased to the point where there were enough to restock the animal in other parts of the continent.

Aberdare National Park covers much of the Treetops salient, a thickly forested area where game viewing is nonetheless excellent. Elephants, buffalo, lions, hyenas, reedbuck, and eland are commonly seen here, both from the viewing decks of Treetops and The Ark lodges and on game drives through the forest and open moorlands.

The moorland areas sit on a high rolling plateau and are covered with heaths and grasses, all with a backdrop of Mt. Kenya and views down into the Rift Valley. Because it offers landscapes and habitats different from the other East African parks, and because visitors have been coming here long enough for the animals to get used to their presence, Aberdare offers a unique game-viewing experience. Even those who prefer the bush life of a tented safari and the involvement of tracking and seeking animals on drives enjoy a night or two in this environment. For the less adventurous traveler, Treetops or The Ark is often the highlight of a safari.

Vultures are a common sight, particularly when a kill is in progress.

North of the town of Nanyuki are the Loldaiga Hills, a rugged ridge of rocky hills overlooking green, rolling grazing lands. The terrain is mixed thornbush, grassland, open woodland, and rocky outcrops.

Although it is privately owned farmland, special tented safaris do camp there using the farm roads and herders' tracks for game drives. Safaris here are so rare that the animals have not grown used to people, but when game is sighted, visitors can be certain of being the only party to see it, instead of jostling for a view amid a crowd of other vehicles. It also provides the opportunity, rare in East Africa, of stalking game on foot.

© Gerry Ellis/Ellis Wildlife Collection

SAFARI ADVENTURE: NOTES FROM A JOURNAL

LOLDAIGA HILLS, KENYA

When the bush plane taxis down the runway of Nairobi's Wilson Airport, you know at last that you're on safari. There is a thrill to the take-off of a bush plane, no matter how often you've done it before; it always signals the beginning of an adventure.

The ragged profile of the Aberdares appears to our left, dark gray and sharp like a row of teeth against the lighter gray sky. They rise from a rumpled patchwork of cultivated fields covering the uneven hillsides at their base. A few small clouds hang suspended below us and the morning

The zebra, among the more commonly seen animals in Africa, is also among the most photogenic.

mists still lie in the valleys to the east. Ahead looms Mt. Kenya, an expanse of jagged rock with spring snow still clinging to its summit.

The clouds end suddenly and the land below is flat, barren, and brown, dotted by a few thorn trees and dark brown squares of plowed fields. Dead ahead lies a narrow brown ribbon in the dry grass—our landing strip. We take direct aim and approach it head-on.

Waiting beside the runway is a green safari vehicle with large windows all around and a pop-up roof hatch. A tall, tanned man in safari shorts strides across the runway as we climb out, ducking to avoid the wing.

"Welcome to A World Apart!" It is Neil Outram, our host, who will be our guide, naturalist, storyteller, and friend throughout the safari. He has a ready laugh, and we like him immediately. The land adventure begins with a ride on a typical Kenya road, only somewhat paved.

The town of Nanyuki lies astride the equator, its main street lined with storefronts, looking like a frontier town from the American West. A short distance beyond, we turn off the main road onto a track that leads through a cattle ranch of several thousand acres, past a thatched village and through a herd of Sahiwel cattle that show their mixed ancestry with the hump of an Indian Brahma and the gentle square face of a Brown Swiss. The countryside becomes hilly and rolling, the road winds and dips through a green riverine valley and across fields of clumpy bush grass and whistling thorn shrubs, white with blossoms.

Ahead, beside a pond and under a grove of Arithrina and wild olive trees is home: a row of

© Gerry Ellis/Ellis Wildlife Collection

neat green tents, each with a canopied veranda, two canvas easy chairs, and a bamboo table in front. There is chilled champagne waiting, and a chance to relax and explore camp before lunch. The tents are good-sized, with high ceilings and plenty of walking space, a locally woven wool rug on the floor, a dressing room and attached wash-tent. It is very comfortable, but wonderfully and unmistakably a bush camp.

The camp staff, tall and elegant in their bright flowing robes, brings dish after dish to the buffet table, carefully covering each one with mosquito netting to keep off the inevitable African flies. Mt. Kenya provides not only a lovely backdrop to lunch, but a pleasant breeze to moderate the mid-day heat.

Lunch could have been served at a fine restaurant, with an assortment of hot and cold dishes that includes subtle seasonings and a variety of cooking styles. There is a steaming savory meatloaf with lightly sautéed red onions, chunks of white-meat chicken in a curried mayonnaise,

noodles with mushrooms and vegetables, avocado with parsley, a salad of diced pineapple with cheese and celery, marinated julienne zucchini, cold sliced meats, fresh baked bread, and a macé-doine of fresh tropical fruits for dessert.

The best times of day for game viewing are just after dawn and late in the afternoon, so camp days are long, with time for an afternoon nap. This is also a good time to catch up on field notes, clean the road dust out of cameras, and stay out of the equatorial sun. Tea is served about 3:30 P.M., a leisurely affair, with fine Kenyan tea and a proper assortment of biscuits. But we are impatient to be off into the hills that surround camp to see what lives in their deepening shadows.

The land is lovely, rolling and lightly forested, with rock outcrops, sharp cliffs, and broad valleys. The brown grasses catch the late afternoon sun and turn gold against the deep green of the thorn and the olive. Herds of zebra, impala, and waterbuck graze, warthogs scamper away, and baboons line up in a ruckus on the rocks.

© Gerry Ellis/Ellis Wildlife Collection

The tawny eagle is a common sight around both kills and campsites in Kenya, and is often seen in the company of vultures.

It doesn't take us long, standing with our heads out the roof hatch, to begin to spot game right along with Neil. The zebras, so distinctive in their dramatic contrasting stripes, blend easily into the light and dark patterns of sunlight and shadow, becoming more difficult to spot than the solid flanks of the antelopes.

There is almost no twilight at the equator. The sun is high, then the sky turns orange, then the sun is gone behind a hill. Shadows disappear and within minutes the sky is deep blue, then black. Driving through the dark we see two flickering orange lights below: the cook fire where our dinner is in progress and the campfire that welcomes us.

It is the typical African campfire made of oddly shaped branches of dead wood, their ends meeting like spokes in a hub, the fire in the center. As the fire burns, the ends are pushed in to provide more fuel. The fire feels good, and we all stand around it warming our hands; because of the altitude, it is surprisingly cool here on the equator.

It was the practice of many British colonials in the days of empire, no matter how remote the post, to dress for dinner and set a proper table each night. While this touch with home and civilization may strike our modern minds as a bit absurd in retrospect, when we step into the dining tent of a proper bush camp it all seems terribly right.

It is a stunning sight, in the middle of the vast,

"There was a wealth of bird-life in the lagoons [of Lake Naivasha.] Small gulls...flew screaming around us. Black and white kingfishers, tiny red-billed kingfishers, with colors so brilliant that they flashed like jewels in the sun, and brilliant green bee-eaters with chestnut breasts perched among the reeds... A giant heron, the Goliath, flew up at our approach; and there were many smaller herons and egrets, white or parti-colored."

Theodore Roosevelt: **African Game Trails,** *1910*

Opposite page: *The grey heron is easily distinguished from other herons by its white neck and crown.*

Pages 76-77: *Zebras are gregarious animals that travel in herds, often with wildebeest.*

There is a permanent tented camp on the largest island, sitting high above the water, and a luxury lodge on the western shore. Each employs ornithologists who conduct walks and boat trips. Although the water of the lake is dull gray from silt, the area is quite scenic with its reeded shores, high-standing islands, and the wall of the Rift Valley rising from one side.

The southernmost of these lakes is Naivasha, only about fifty miles (80 km) from Nairobi. It is a freshwater lake set in rich farming country and has even more bird species than Baringo. Waterbirds, including fish eagles, ospreys, herons, egrets, coots and crakes, nest in the reeds and low shrubs along the shore, where visitors can approach quite closely by boat. The lake is also home to about five hundred hippos.

At the hotel at Lake Naivasha, raised walkways and observation blinds bring guests closer to the birds. For the dedicated birder, Lake Naivasha could well be the highlight of a Kenya safari.

Crescent Island, in the center of the lake, is a private reserve and home to zebras, gazelles, and other animals. Since there are no predators, the island is a safe place for walking.

THE SERENGETI

Within the 5,600 square miles (9,032 sq km) that make up the Serengeti National Park lives the largest concentration of wild game on the continent. The numbers of migrating animals are staggering: 1.5 million wildebeests, one-quarter million zebras. With that many animals, a head count becomes not only impossible, but inconsequential.

Where there are grazers predators follow, so it is not surprising that the Serengeti is one of Africa's best places to see lions. Leopards and cheetahs, while not as easy to spot, are abundant there too.

Located on the northern border of Tanzania, the Serengeti adjoins the Masai Mara in Kenya. The animals, of course, recognize no borders and travel between the two countries with far less difficulty than the tourists who follow them. In fact, human travelers cannot cross by road between the two parks even though a road does exist. They must go all the way east to Namanga, through Arusha and back up to the Kenya-Tanzania border.

"The big glowing ball of the sun has disappeared behind the horizon and the plains game are breathing freely after the heat of the day. From the great spaces you hear the monotonous bellowing of the wildebeest; by the thousands they are slowly trekking northwards following the new tender pastures . . . Every time I come down here to the Serengeti I get just as impressed and enchanted as I did on my first trip by the enormous quantity of game. The number must be limited, but nowhere else in the world will you, within an area of this size, find such an amazing display of wildlife."

Bror Blixen, **The Africa Letters**, *1988*

Although Serengeti National Park is best known for its annual migrations, when animals thunder past in a steady stream for days on end, the game viewing here is excellent at other times as well. It is difficult to predict the exact dates of the migration, but in general, the great herds will be in the southern part of the park between December and May when the migration begins. During the next month the animals move north, pass Seronera, and reach the Masai Mara in mid-July. From then until the short rains begin in October, the heaviest concentrations are in the Serengeti and Masai Mara. The return trip begins in early October, and the herds are back in the Lake Ndutu area by December.

The Serengeti landscape varies from a vast flat plain to rolling savannah and hills. Breaking the flatness are hills of rounded rock, called kopjes, which burst forth on the horizon and look like great mountains from a distance. In reality, they loom by the roadside, only relatively small outcrops after all.

The kopjes often have trees growing on or around them and are favorite spots for predators to lurk while they view the surrounding grasslands. Toward the north the kopjes grow larger and more dramatic. Lobo Lodge, the northernmost of the two lodges in the park, is on the crest of one of these, beautifully built on several levels among giant cliffs and boulders. The view down onto the plain is of rolling grasslands, open woodland, pools and rock outcrops—strewn with grazing buffalo, zebras, wildebeests, elephants, and giraffes. It is one of East Africa's loveliest views.

Both Seronera and Lobo are government-run hotels; the only other accommodation is at Ndutu, a private tented camp, just outside the park on the southeast. Travel between lodges is by van or land cruiser, which can be engaged in Arusha or arranged in advance by an outfitter in Nairobi.

One of the pleasures of the Serengeti is the element of surprise. In the midst of a flat and empty plain, a pack of wild dogs may suddenly trot up the road. A pool at a river crossing may be full of hippos, and on the shore, a baby completely out of the water stands looking on. A long, spotted tail hanging limply from a tree announces a leopard sleeping above. Lions sit not ten feet (3 m) from the road and calmly regard stopped vehicles.

The Serengeti has a good balance of visitors and wildlife—enough of the former so that the animals have grown less shy, but not so many that it becomes overcrowded. Its major drawback is that travel is limited to the few roads, and they don't always lead to where the game is. Especially in the north, the great herds often disperse into areas far out of sight of any road.

© Silliman Rogers

Above: *The terrain of the northern Serengeti, near Lobo, is more rolling, marked by towering kopjes.*

Opposite page: *A long tail hanging limply from a tree announces this lioness taking a rest above.*

SAFARI ADVENTURE: NOTES FROM A JOURNAL

THE SERENGETI, TANZANIA:

You have to love the wild places of the earth to find the haunting, compelling beauty of the Serengeti Plain. Except during the rainy season (January through April), when daily downpours render its roads impassable, the Serengeti is the soft buff-green of dust and dry grass.

The landscape is broken by the brown-gray of thornbush, dark brown of rocks, and the deep green, almost black crowns of the umbrella thorn in the valleys. Above is an expanse of pale blue sky that melts into haze at the horizon. The plain and the sky are so overwhelmingly big that one vehicle seems very small and alone.

The land surrounding the Serengeti's borders is even more barren, overgrazed by Masai cattle, which are not allowed in the park. Only in the valleys and on their slopes are there trees or grass. Thorn trees there grow tall enough for giraffes to browse in their tops, and we stop to watch them move sedately from one to another. Groups of Masai children in bright beaded collars jump up and down beside the road, but apart from the children and the giraffes, there is little sign of life.

Past the dust-filled track to Olduvai Gorge, the land becomes even more flat and barren. The tiny tufts of grass are widely separated by dry gray dust. We see a group of Masai herdsmen standing in the scant shade of a thorn with their cattle, and

Groups of Masai girls frequently stand by the road-side in Tanzania, wearing collars of bright beads.

we wonder what these poor beasts find to eat in this land. Here and there are bleached white skulls of buffalo or cattle. The rusted skeleton of a bus lies on its side, far from the road, as though it had been dragged there by hyena and stripped bare by vultures. These are not encouraging sights.

Ahead looms the gate to the Serengeti National Park, and immediately the vegetation changes. It is not lush, but a sage-green grass covers the ground evenly, growing out of an underlying mat of grass, instead of from dust. The land is still unbroken by bush or tree, but it is less forbidding.

In the unwavering sunlight, distant mountains float above the horizonlike islands in a lake of heat waves. To the west there is no horizon, no sign of the line where earth becomes sky.

The park headquarters is set in the trees at the base of a kopje, like an oasis in the midst of this thirsty land. The ground and trees are covered with flocks of brilliant blue superb starlings. They are like Hildebrandt's starlings; but without the white band separating the red and the blue on their breasts. Even in the shade they glow with iridescent, electric color, and they fill the air with their chirping.

Beyond, a gazelle grazes by the roadside and a silver-backed jackal stops to watch us pass. The jackal is so doglike in appearance and actions that it is easy to see why it is thought to be the ancestor of the domestic dog. A good hunter and retriever, perhaps it joined early man on the hunt.

Large birds strut in the grass: the secretary bird and the kori bustard. As we move deeper into the park, the animal life grows more plentiful—a herd of gazelles, more jackals, then, suddenly, as we round a kopje, the plain ahead is black and moving in front of us. There, in a long, thick line, are the wildebeests, the first wave of the migration from the Masai Mara. We drive on, and as far as we can possibly see there are wildebeests and zebras.

Some are moving, some grazing, and we stop to watch a herd of zebras by a pool. Zebras seem always to drink in a row, the stripes of their faces blending into a pattern and their round noses evenly spaced in the water. Viewed from behind as an even row of rumps, each has its own mirror image of stripes, bisected by a tail whose black and white lines are so evenly spaced and slanted that it looks like a braid with a tassled end.

I love to watch zebras, not only for their unique pattern of black and white lines, but because they seem to drink like vacuum cleaners. They show no sign of lapping or scooping the water into their mouths, just a steady, soundless, motionless slurp. The muzzles in their neat row barely move

Burchell's zebras are the most commonly seen wildlife throughout East Africa; Grevy's zebras are numerous only in Samburu Park.

© Gerry Ellis/Ellis Wildlife Collection

© Gerry Ellis/Ellis Wildlife Collection

until one group of animals leaves to make way for another group. I think my favorite image of Africa is of a herd of zebras drinking at a pool or standing in the tall grass under a spreading umbrella thorn. It is an image repeated throughout Africa, from Mt. Kenya to the Transvaal, and I never tire of it.

The grass grows taller and greener near the Seronera River, and a group of topis grazes beside the road. There are so many of these different species of antelope that we are never quite sure we have them straight. Just as we are certain of one from its size and markings, a ranger corrects us— we have spotted a younger animal whose markings have not matured. But the topi's rich color and dark legs make it easy to remember, just as the dark stripe on the side of a Thompson's gazelle make it easy to identify.

We know that near this river is a favorite place for leopards, who hunt in the evening as the grazers come to drink and spend their days stretched in the high branches of the thorn trees. We watch these trees as we pass under them, hoping for a glimpse of a long tail hanging below the foliage. We think we have spotted one, but it turns out to be the leg of a gazelle, dragged there by a leopard and hung over a limb to keep it out of reach of other predators until it could be finished.

Not a mile from the Seronera Lodge, we do spot one, a real tail this time, in a tree quite near the road. No animal is so completely relaxed in its repose as the leopard. As they spread out, high in a tree, they are safe in the knowledge that nothing will attack them. This leopard lies with his body draped the length of a limb, head and shoulder supported by a forking branch, one rear leg and tail hanging off. We watch for nearly half an hour; the leopard stirs occasionally, looking at us, then closes its eyes and shifts its position slightly before going back to sleep.

Grant's gazelles are most frequently found in Meru, Samburu, and Tsavo National Parks, and in the Loldaiga Hills near Mt. Kenya.

Leopards are not common in the Serengeti because there are so many lions, the leopard's only competitor and predator. They avoid the tall grasses where the lion hides, but here near the river there are large trees where the lion cannot disturb them.

For the sheer quantity of its animals, even when the migration is not in progress, the Serengeti is impressive. In a single morning we have seen fourteen mammal and twenty bird species. Toward Lobo Lodge, near the Kenya frontier, the land grows more rolling and varied, with more trees and larger kopjes. Giraffes are plentiful again as the trees grow taller and thicker. We see

another topi, this time with her young, which we would have mistaken for a hartebeest had we not seen the mother.

Two white-headed vultures stand at the top of a dead tree, looking intently north. Very soon we see another pair circling in the air ahead and we suspect that there is a kill in progress. We are learning to read the land.

A wildebeest is difficult for hyena to bring down. They are strong and they fight fiercely, using their sharp horns and hooves. But those weakened from injury, or old and unable to run, are an easier mark. When one is stricken with the curious "circling disease," which causes older

animals to run in circles, it is only a matter of waiting and annoying the beast until it is tired.

It is this kind of kill that we find in progress. The wildebeest is down and already savagely torn, but gets up and drags itself away, still moving in circles, until brought to the ground again. Fighting on, the gray beast tries to impale a hyena with his horn, but is attacked by another from behind. The predators back off a little and wait.

A cloud of vultures has assembled, drawn by the signal of the two we saw circling earlier. As the hyenas are engrossed in their work, the vultures move forward, joining in until the hyena chases them away. The birds retreat a few yards—then they immediately begin to close in again.

A kill is not a pretty sight, but it is part of the endless cycle of life and death in the Serengeti. Each death provides food and therefore life, and there is nothing wasted.

We marked the spot of this one so that we could return in the morning. When we did, there was nothing there. No sign of the struggle, no darkened place in the grass to show where the kill took place. Predators and scavengers had carried the bones away to finish in privacy, eventually eating those, too, or reducing them to splinters. Even the skull, the one part of the kill that is not consumed, had been dragged away.

Wildebeest are common throughout East and South Africa, traveling in herds which often number in the thousands.

THE NGORONGORO CRATER

Unlike any of Africa's other great game-viewing destinations, this ancient crater supports an entire ecosystem of large animals that make it their permanent home. A few of these animals move up the slopes to forage and the elephants come and go over the rim, but most stay within the crater floor.

A caldera is caused by the collapse of a crater cone and in the case of the Ngorongoro Crater, it left a hole twelve miles (19 km) in diameter surrounded by a rim more than 2,000 feet (700 m) high. The floor is a vast savannah with a soda lake, freshwater pools, an open forest of yellow-barked acacia trees, and several marshy areas. The walls of the rim are forested—quite densely at the top, where a covering of low clouds provides fairly even moisture.

Opposite page: Hippos spend most of their time in the water, and travel on land only at night to feed.

Below: The walk of a lioness may seem leisurely, almost careless, but she is always alert, especially if her cubs are near.

In this habitat live all of the "Big Five" game animals (elephant, buffalo, rhinoceros, lion, and leopard), except for the leopard, which finds better hunting on the forested rim. Grazers and predators, plus wetland and soda lake bird-life, are found in a balance that pretty well maintains itself. Only the rhinoceros is in serious danger of extinction here, with its herd down to twenty-five animals, a very small gene pool.

Few places offer so many species in such a small area, or wildlife so accustomed to the presence of vehicles. It is possible to drive into the middle of a herd of wildebeests and zebras, and to within a few yards of a rhinoceros. In fact, it is one of the few places where it is very likely that this rare creature will be spotted. There are hippopotamuses in the freshwater pools, and the soda lake is host to flamingos and pelicans.

© Gerry Ellis/Ellis Wildlife Collection

© Gerry Ellis/Ellis Wildlife Collection

"The Masai, we were told, were slaughtering an increasing number of rhino [in the Ngorongoro Crater]. When detected, they always pleaded self defence: actually one can be sure that other motives were at work—not only does a dead rhino provide hard cash from the sale of its horn, but its killing (with a spear, remember!) provides a gratifying outlet for Masai courage and virility."

Julian Huxley, quoted in Wild Lives of Africa, 1963

Photography is easy, not only because the animals are used to cars, but because there is very little vegetation to obscure them. There is enough tall grass to give some sport to lion "hunting" and enough lions to make the chance of success fairly high.

Although travel in Tanzania is both aggravating and bone-jarring, it is worth considerable effort and hardship to spend even a day in the Ngorongoro Crater. There are four lodges of varying quality on the rim, two of which look right down into the crater. Tented safaris set up their camps under the shade of the acacia forest on the floor of the crater, and their guests are the only visitors allowed inside the crater after sunset.

Outside the crater, the Ngorongoro Conservation District covers the area between the crater and the Serengeti National Park. This area is gray and dusty from overgrazing—the Masai herd their cattle here—but stands of dark green umbrella thorn and a rolling terrain break the monotony and give it a wild beauty. The road is unimproved and often little more than loose dust and gravel over a rocky ledge. Giraffes, wildebeests, zebras, and gazelles graze and browse by the roadside.

Pages 88-89: *The African jacana is often called the lily trotter because of its ability to walk along the floating vegetation of its watery habitat.*

Opposite page: *The Masai giraffe is a common sight in those parts of the Masai Mara and Serengeti where there are trees.*

Above: *The rhino population throughout Africa is alarmingly low. In some places there are not enough left to assure a proper gene pool.*

SAFARI ADVENTURE: NOTES FROM A JOURNAL

THE NGORONGORO CRATER, TANZANIA:

Along the wall of the Great Rift Valley, the dust is a rich terra-cotta color and the bright green of the farms contrasts against it sharply in the late afternoon sun. Fields of wheat turn amber in the golden light and giant baobabs and umbrella acacias are dark silhouettes against the deepening sky and purple mountains. The road as we ascend the rim winds sharply, and is pitted, rock-strewn, and washed away. It is little more than a track made wide enough for the infrequent cars and the buses packed three and four to a seat that carry workers between Arusha and the farms.

The long trip from the rim down into the Ngorongoro Crater in the morning is an aggravatingly slow trip on a narrow, washed-out road.

Dark begins to fall as we approach the crater. We can see little except for the faint lights of two villages far below in the Rift Valley and a flickering campfire on the crater floor below us on the other side. The road runs along the narrow rim, and we imagine what the daylight views must be.

A buffalo appears suddenly in the track ahead, a great dark hulk as startled as we are. He faces us evenly, his wide spreading horns meeting in the center of his forehead like thick hair parted in the middle. This part and the sweeping upward curve of the horns give him a slightly ridiculous look, as though he sports a bouffant hairstyle from the 1960s. He turns and moves off into the underbrush, disappearing completely as he leaves the range of our headlights. The entire world, except for the track before us, is lost in darkness and smells richly of woodsmoke blended with African dust—a smell that seems to unite the entire sub-Saharan expanse of the continent.

The Ngorongoro Wildlife Lodge is spread along the rim of the crater, just inside its inner edge, and each room has a view down into the crater floor. The huge lounge has the easy ambience of a ski lodge, a big fireplace at one end, a bar along one side, and comfortable chairs set in groups for guests to exchange experiences and safari tales. The dinner menu offers several choices and we try zebra stew. In this form, zebra meat is much like beef, although it more resembles venison when grilled.

The lodges here, as is often true in Tanzania, do not have their own vehicles, and our van, more comfortable than a four-wheel-drive vehicle for long days on the road, cannot navigate the steep

© Stillman-Rogers

narrow track into the crater. So our outfitter has arranged for a land cruiser and guide to meet us just after daybreak.

The amazing thing is that these plans were made many weeks ago in the United States, and relayed to Arusha via Nairobi. Arusha is a half day's drive away from the lodge, but weeks later, in the gray mist that covers the crater rim in the morning, our vehicle and guide arrive on time. Having coped for years with how things usually work (or don't) in Africa, we regard this as a minor miracle.

Except for the few Masai and the private tented safaris, no one can spend the night inside the crater, and vehicles cannot descend from the rim until after 7:00 A.M. It is frustrating, since we are used to being among the wildlife during these precious early hours when they are their most active and visible. Our progress in the long parade of jeeps and cruisers is painfully slow, as we drive down the rutted, rock-strewn trail.

Finally at the bottom, 2,000 feet (700 m) below our lodge, now lost in a cloud, we join all the other vehicles as they stop to open roof hatches and photograph the three bored Masai boys who pose, then assess a fee from everyone nearby with a camera. There are too many vehicles, too many people with loud voices calling from car to car.

It is at this point that another couple, alone in their car, look over at us, smiling, and give us the high sign. We signal back, each grateful that our outfitters had insisted on exclusive safaris for us. We might have to share the crater, but not a car.

Inside the Ngorongoro Crater is a complete ecosystem; most species never leave its confining rim.

93

At last we pull off, asking our driver to take another road than that taken by the rest of the vehicles, moving in a long procession like a circus parade of elephants. Almost immediately we are in the middle of a herd of wildebeests. We stop and spend half an hour watching them drink, eat, and move about us in the company of a large group of zebras. These animals are frequent companions, their symbiotic relationship protecting them both. The zebra, with keen vision, is good at looking out for predators; it eats the tender top grasses. The wildebeest sees poorly, but has sharp ears; it eats the coarse bottom grasses. Together, zebra and wildebeest can graze more safely and do not have to compete for food.

The wildebeest is such a sorrowful-looking creature that his shaggy brown beard, oversized head, and hangdog expression remind us of a cartoon version of a prehistoric mammoth-goat.

Reluctant to leave the experience of sitting inside a herd, we move on at last, coming upon a small gazelle grazing alone. We approach slowly, turn off the engine, and watch. We are so close we can hear the grass tearing as she pulls it with her teeth. The only other sound in the crater is the wind rustling in the dry grass. Nearby, in a dry pan are more Grant's gazelles and hartebeests.

We know that we have a better chance of seeing rhinos here than in any other place in East Africa, so we head for the part of the crater they favor. We see several—some grazing, a pair lying together in the dust, and an unusually pale female with a two-year-old baby. Slow to develop, the young rhino will stay two more years with the mother.

A pair of buffalo watch us, and as we stop, several more join them. At times like this, I wonder who is viewing whom and feel vaguely as though we'd been brought in to entertain the troops.

Wildebeest and zebra herds frequently travel and graze together. The good eyesight of the zebra and the sharp ears of the wildebeest protect the animals from predators.

© Gerry Ellis/Ellis Wildlife Collection

Lions are fairly common in the crater, which we might have expected, because of the great quantities of lion food we have seen grazing. Their habits and coloring make them hard to spot, since they hunt in the early morning and retire to the brown grass for the day to sleep. But we are lucky enough to see a pride still busy with a kill, and a male, his mane and face still red with blood, standing atop a hummock watching the females and younger males finish off a zebra.

Not far away the rest of the zebra herd grazes, but there are two lookouts watching the busy lions. As we watch, we realize what is missing. There are no vultures. Usually at a fresh kill, the vultures arrive in flocks before the quarry is down, and stand by, waiting, or circle in the air to signal others.

By lunchtime the cloud has completely evaporated from the rim, and the sky is deep blue overhead. The sloping sides of the crater are visible all around as we retire to a freshwater pool surrounded by bright green reeds—the home of a pod of hippos who gather to watch us eat.

I stand up to watch a hippo, and a huge kite swoops down from above me, snatching the sandwich as I lift it to my mouth. He leaves me with a cut under my eye and a long scratch on my hand from the talons. I finish lunch in the safety of the vehicle and watch the hippos through an open window.

Such oases dot the crater. At the far end we find a vast field of green reeds, and we park on a grassy mound to watch an elephant munch his way toward us, progressing slowly through the tall reeds until he stands almost beside us. On the other side of us is a sideshow, a clear pool containing about twenty hippos. They submerge with a great splash, then rise to watch me, their bugeyes, furrowed brows, and little round ears all that show above the surface. They dive again and lunge out with open mouths, roll over completely and disappear. Baby hippos swim alongside, mimicking the antics of the adults.

We spend an hour here, the sun sliding lower, watching the hippos and elephant as the afternoon light catches the shine of the reeds and reflects off the rippling water. The crater walls become a soft pastel blue and we finally leave to cross the crater floor while the sun still hangs above its rim.

At the far end, where the exit road begins its hair-raising ascent (it is easy to see why we didn't come down by this more direct route) is a glade of tall yellow-barked acacias. Under their filtered shade is a camp, its green tents in a long row like the one we'd left at Loldaiga. The late sun accentuates the yellow of the tree trunks and the first cooling touch of evening with its distinctive earthy fragrances moves in.

We decide that next time we will camp here in the crater, but we are pleased with our first visit. Nowhere else have we seen so much game so close and in such a short time. What the crater lacks in sport (we didn't have to hunt at all) it makes up in the amount of wildlife and the opportunity to mingle with it so closely.

Left: *When he has eaten his fill, the male lion looks for a place to sleep and leaves the rest of the carcass to lionesses and cubs.*

Below: *Hippos avoid the heat of the day by remaining mostly submerged in pools such as this one in the Ngorongoro Crater.*

© Stillman Rogers

TARANGIRE

South of Arusha, Tarangire National Park sits on the Tarangire River, which flows throughout the dry season. As other water supplies dry up, animals move closer and closer to the river. Herds of zebras, wildebeests, waterbuck, and large herds of elephants gather near this water source from May until the rains begin in October.

The only accommodations are a tented camp set along the ridge of a steep hill overlooking the river and an open landscape that slopes gently up on the other side dotted with baobab and thorn trees. At any time of day, the view from the terrace here is filled with elephants and other animals. Unfortunately, the rhinoceros population has been poached almost to extinction, but Tarangire is one of the few places that visitors can get close enough to photograph baby elephants at play.

The landscape in Tarangire is full of rolling hills, with giant baobab trees, acacias and open grasslands giving it an entirely different atmosphere from the Serengeti. The camp, too, has an informal friendly air, far different from the impersonal Serengeti lodges. Game drives can be made

"Great baobab trees dotted the landscape, which otherwise consisted of dense bush with thorn trees and bayonet grass. To me these giant baobabs do not quite look real, and are no more similar to other trees than the giraffe and rhino resemble other animals."

Bror Blixen, The Africa Letters, *1988*

© Gerry Ellis/Ellis Wildlife Collection

Opposite page: *Giant baobab trees tower above the savannah in Tanzania's Tarangire National Park.*

Left: *Tarangire Safari Lodge is possibly the best place in East Africa to watch the antics of baby elephants at close range.*

in lodge vehicles or in the travel vans by which visitors arrive. Sunsets here are often spectacular; the sun drops behind the Rift escarpment, with the great baobabs silhouetted in black across the orange sky.

Tarangire is a pleasant camp for a longer stay, although a trip there can also be combined with one to nearby Lake Manyara. This large alkaline lake and the park around it support several different habitats and vegetation zones. Forests of fig and ebony trees are dense and shaded, while grasslands and more open acacia forests provide better views. The dense undergrowth in the forest near the water may be the attraction for the park's most interesting residents, the tree-climbing lions.

Elephants, hippos, and buffalo are plentiful on the shores of Manyara, and many of the animals are year-round residents. Not far from Arusha, this park is popular when the rainy season makes travel up the Rift and crater walls difficult. Because of the marshy areas around the lake, birdlife is excellent—more than 350 species have been reported.

Small birds such as the oxpecker keep the hides of buffalo free of insects, and so are often found where these animals are plentiful.

© Gerry Ellis/Ellis Wildlife Collection

THE OKAVANGO DELTA

The inland delta of the Okavango River, unlike the great deltas of the Nile or the Mississippi, does not spread the waters of the river into the sea, but rather into land. The rushing waters of the Okavango River flow not to the Atlantic Ocean, only 150 miles (240 km) away, but eastward, across the continent toward the Indian Ocean. The waters never reach the Indian Ocean. In fact, they don't even come close, but fan out instead into a vast and intricate web of streams, waterways, and lagoons that is eventually swallowed up by the thirst of the Kalahari sands.

In this delta is one of the few almost totally unspoiled environments on earth. The safari camps in the area are made up of clusters of tents set around open-sided dining areas and reed-enclosed camp kitchens. No camps are permanent, and the government of Botswana is reluctant to permit any more incursion into this watery wilderness.

The small number of camps and their remote locations make the Okavango even more irresistible as a safari destination. While exploring the delta it is rare to meet another vehicle—even one from your own camp of seven or eight tents. Game "drives" are often by *mokoro*, a dugout log canoe, or a more watertight modern version. Poled silently through the reeds and waterlilies, these lovely boats bring observers and photographers to within a few feet of nesting water birds.

Animal life is abundant on the islands, with herds of elephant, red lechwe, tsessebe (sassaby), sable, impala, buffalo, and zebra. Lions and leopards lie in wait for these creatures, or snooze in the middle of the day. Hippos keep trails clear through the waterways, making paths for boats to follow, and the banks of pools and rivers are a favorite sunning place for crocodiles.

Birdlife is especially plentiful—both water and land species reside in the Okavango, and others migrate from Europe's winter to nest there. Palms, ebony, sausage trees, mopane, marula, and the flowering raintree join the ever-present thorn in a terrain well watered by floods that move slowly into the region during its own dry season.

No vast savannahs mark the Okavango, but there are island habitats of grassland, salt pans, reedy pools, bands of deep forest, low thornbush, and mopane scrublands, and entire areas of forest hacked and toppled by the local wrecking crew—the elephants. The terrain of the Okavango and its infinite wildlife never grows monotonous, and each camp offers new habitats to explore.

*Found from southern Kenya through the Transvaal
and into Namibia, the impala is the most commonly
seen animal in Kruger National Park.*

SAFARI ADVENTURE: NOTES FROM A JOURNAL

THE OKAVANGO DELTA:

The land below us is patterned in circles of brown and white and swirling, green paisleylike designs. We are flying so low that we can see herds of elephant and buffalo, and even antelope, from the bush plane. Lines radiate from the dusty circles—the trails of animals that came to drink when these were water holes during the rainy season. Now, at the end of the dry season, the only water is in the main channels, changing in course and even in direction as the waters seep throughout the delta. The green swirls are the long, green grasses just beneath the water's surface—the only clue to the direction of the water's slow flow.

Pom Pom Camp has the perfect setting, as it faces a lagoon alive with birds, choked with lavender water lilies, and bobbing with hippos. Huge trees shade its seven tents, and there is just a stirring of breeze to temper the afternoon heat. The lagoon ends in a wall of tall reeds that are bright green in the sun and hide the channels that wind through them.

The veranda of our tent faces the water, and from it we watch a pod of hippos bobbing and rolling like gray beach balls. A *mokoro* slides into view through the lilies and the hippo heads all pop up at once, a line of little eyes watching.

Birdlife in the Okavango Delta is even more abundant than at Kenya's Lake Baringo Island Camp, already famous for its birds. Here they flit, fly, hop, swim, soar, and walk everywhere; they even come quite close and pose for pictures.

The best time to enjoy the birds is between brunch and teatime, a span of three hours or so when everyone has retired to their tents for a nap. The camp is silent except for the birds and the splash of an occasional fish jumping for a fly. The

The yellow-billed stork frequents shallow waters throughout East Africa.

hippos have stopped their roaring huffle and retired to the shade of the tall reeds at the far side of the lagoon.

A pair of pygmy geese float among the lily pads not fifteen feet (4.5 m) from me, and a bright blue starling hops around my chair leaving a spiderweb of tracks in the powdery gray dust. An African jacana walks on the water, steps from lily pad to lily pad, stays on each just as long as the surface tension of the water bears his weight, then moves lightly to the next. The local name for these translates quite appropriately to "lily trotter."

There is a snag of dead wood jutting out of the water just in front of the camp. It is perfectly placed—there is usually a large water bird perched there drying its wings or watching for fish below—and each new guest in turn accuses the camp managers, Cecil and Brigitte, of putting it there just for effect.

In the morning, we leave at seven by *mokoro*, cross the glassy surface of the lagoon, then maneuver through the narrow, reed-lined channels past palm-filled islands that explode with cormorants as we pass. We come at last to an island where we moor and go ashore through a tangle of shining grass. We walk through thornbush, under large mopane trees, across grassy fields and over the bases of abandoned termite mounds. We investigate elephant tracks and the bone-white droppings of hyena.

Someone smells smoke and we turn to see a column of flame not 100 yards (90 m) behind us, where we had just been walking.

Apparently someone in the group we were with has carelessly dropped a match and the dry grass goes up like tinder. We are close enough to hear the sickening crackle of dry wood and grass catching. A breeze blows the smoke directly toward us, which means that we are in the path of a now un-

© Gerry Ellis/Ellis Wildlife Collection

controllable bush fire. We are a distance from the *mokoros*, which rest on the other side of thick thornbush. The thornbush and tall, coarse grass alternately catch at our clothes and trip us as we hurry. The smoke and the sound of the fire follow us, and for once, we wish that the cooling breeze were not blowing across the bush.

We finally reach the *mokoros*. As we slide through the grass toward open water, we can see the smoke rising over an increasing area. All afternoon a haze of smoke hangs over the land, and as dark comes, we can see the glow of two fires, the center section having burned out and the fire spread toward both sides of the island. All night the horizon glows with a wavering orange light.

■

Machaba Camp sits on the Kwai River at a point where the elephants come to water several times a

The cape teal is a commonly found species on the soda lakes of East Africa.

day. It is easy to understand, even in the short drive from the airstrip to camp, why an environment can support only so many elephants. Shattered trees lie everywhere, splintered snags that look as though they've been left by a giant lawn mower, and entire trees have been stripped clean of their bark.

The land at the end of the long dry season is still green along the rivers, and the bridge over the River Kwai still lies somewhat below the surface of the water. The higher areas are covered with brown grass, and the dry leaves of the mopane rustle in the breeze. The raintree is heavy with fragrant purple flower clusters, and the leadwood is in leaf. Even now the landscape is varied, and seems less harsh than other African environments because of the green.

A stand of giraffes is pruning the tops of the thorn trees, and Cowboy, our Tswana ranger, carefully positions our open vehicle for the perfect camera angle, so the sun hits their tawny rust-and-cream coats. We can watch their slightly silly, camel-like faces as they munch. It is surprising how graceful these animals are, even when they run. Isak Dinesen described them as ladies in flowing dresses, which may seem odd to those who have never seen them move in the bush. They are stately and full of grace, especially in light of their knobby knees, long legs, and triangular bodies. To watch them run is like watching a film in slow motion. They glide so smoothly and cover such a distance, moving so little in the process that their motion appears to be totally effortless.

Giraffes blend into the forest quickly. Their legs and necks are easy to mistake for tree trunks, and their colors quickly blend into the blotchy pattern of sunshine and shadow. Even in open terrain they are easily lost from view.

It is not so easy, however, for elephants to hide. Since they have knocked down so much of the forest, their large, almost black bulk is easy to spot in the open lands and along the rivers, and since they have no predators, they are perfectly comfortable in the open.

For me, it is the most fun to watch the elephants in the water, spraying themselves, rolling in the cool mud, and standing knee deep in the water nibbling on water lilies. When they emerge, their thick hides black from the water and mud, they scoop up great trunkfuls of dry dust and powder themselves all over with it, spraying it in a cloud.

■

The approach to Shindi Island is spectacular. A bush plane flies guests to its small airstrip deep in the Okavanga, but here it is a boat, not a four-by-four, that awaits passengers. For forty-five

Opposite page: *The red-billed hornbill is easily distinguished from the yellow-billed species by its bright red bill.*

Below: *Masai giraffes, more common than the reticulated species, have uneven splotches with irregular edges.*

© Gerry Ellis/Ellis Wildlife Collection

minutes, the boat winds through a maze of tunnels, plumes of papyrus towering overhead against the blue sky. Sometimes the channel opens out into a river or lagoon. Other times, the narrow channel will seem to disappear completely, making the boat appear to be heading for a solid wall of papyrus, the narrow channel entrance visible at the last moment, as the boat noses into it.

At Shindi Island, everything revolves around the best ways to see the abundance of wildlife with which the area is blessed. There are many options: fishing trips, *mokoro* rides, game and bird viewing by power launch, an all-day trip to another island to see a herd of sable antelope, or a fascinating excursion to the rookeries of malibu storks, spoonbills, cormorants, and other waterfowl.

This last trip takes us to within a few feet of the nests in the low bushes that grow along the banks. The ride back at sunset shows the delta's waterways in a different light, with the sun picking up the bright green of the new papyrus, the deep russet of their old plumes, and the water reflecting the sky. In every direction the sky is a different color, from pink to orange to pale lavender, as the setting sun hits different layers of cloud.

After the morning game drive, we travel by boat to a spot not far from camp, where breakfast is waiting in a grassy clearing near the water. An upturned *mokoro* is the buffet table, from which is served chilled champagne and a hearty farmer's omelet baked in a tin oven. The food service in all these delta camps is even more surprising when we remember that each item we eat, and every ingredient and utensil used in its preparation, must be ordered by radio and flown from Maun—a small outpost town itself. The complete isolation of these camps is easy to forget in the hospitable comfort of their compounds.

© Gerry Ellis/Ellis Wildlife Collection

CHOBE

Lying northeast of the Okavango Delta and barely touching it at one corner, is Botswana's second great natural wilderness area, Chobe National Park. Its northern border is the Chobe River, which will join the Zambezi shortly before it drops over the cliffs at Victoria Falls. Chobe consists of more than 30,000 square miles (48,387 sq km) of protected wilderness, cut by few roads.

The river habitat along the banks of the Chobe is low, grassy marshland rising to open forest and thornbush. Farther west are the Linyati Swamps and the Savuti Channel. The Linyati Swamps are a marshy area overgrown with papyrus, a habitat much like the low, wet areas of the Okavango. Game, once plentiful in the Savuti, dispersed somewhat during the decade of drought in the 1980s. Even without the plethora it once offered, it is better for watching wildlife than many other more popular areas, especially for lions.

The most popular area of Chobe, both for ease of access and for its variety of big game, is the Serondela region along the river only 50 miles (80 km) from Victoria Falls. Regular overland transportation by bus is available between the Chobe Game Lodge and Victoria Falls.

The elephant herds in the Serondela region of Chobe are among the largest in Africa, as are the enormous herds of Cape buffalo. It is actually common to see up to a hundred buffalo at a time. Puku and the Chobe bushbuck (a subspecies found only in the Serondela region), kudu, waterbuck, and lechwe all frequent the riverbanks, along with hippos, monkeys, baboons, and banded mongoose. The grounds of the Chobe Game Lodge are constantly under attack by warthogs, which dig in the lawns to uproot insect grubs. Lions are seen here, but not nearly as frequently as at Savuti.

The area along the Chobe River is a favorite one for birders, with hundreds of species around the Chobe Game Lodge alone. Hammerkop, louries, vultures, guinea fowl, storks, hornbills, and rollers are everywhere, along with a multitude of smaller more elusive birds. Game viewing seems, unfortunately, second priority here, with guests seated several abreast in large open trucks. Sundowner cruises, however, offer a good view of river life in the evening as animals come down to the shore to drink. Savuti has a tented camp with more emphasis on game viewing.

"As dawn breaks, the river takes on various shades of pink; there is a pervading tranquility, and you feel completely at one with nature."

Clive Walker: **Above Africa**, *1989*

Pages 110-111: *Elephants, such as this finely tusked specimen, are a prime target of poachers.*

The masked weaver is just one of the many species that have been spotted in Kruger National Park.

© Gerry Ellis/Ellis Wildlife Collection

KRUGER NATIONAL PARK AND THE SABIE-SAND

The landscapes of the eastern Transvaal are low, rolling, grassy savannahs with thorn and leadwood trees, broken by a web of riverine valleys with narrow bands of thick forest. Rock kopjes, reed-lined pools, and wide, sandy riverbeds give even greater variety as well as an increased range of habitats for wildlife.

Larger than the state of Massachusetts, Kruger has been a national park since 1926, and is home to more species of wildlife than any other African game sanctuary. There are 130 species of mammals and over 450 species of birds. Well over 8,000 elephants, nearly 30,000 buffalo, 25,000 zebras, and a staggering 95,000 impala are just the beginning of the census list.

The gerunek is uniquely equipped for survival; its long neck and legs enable it to reach vegetation unavailable to shorter animals.

Kruger, with the neighboring private lands of the Sabie-Sand Reserves, forms one of Africa's richest game-viewing areas, and is an example of wildlife management and conservation that has provided a model for other African nations slower to come to grips with habitat encroachment and poaching.

The two staging points for safaris are Nelspruit and Skakuza, both with airports, and easy to reach from Johannesburg. Most of the Sabie-Sand Lodges have their own airstrips for small planes.

Game viewing in Kruger National Park is by private vehicle; these must remain on roads and be covered. Those arriving by air can rent cars or, as is more common, take advantage of a courier/guide service. With Garth MacFarlane Safaris, after being met at the airport by rangers, visitors tour Kruger in "combies"—special vans with oversized windows for a full view of game.

These MacFarlane safaris stop at one or more of the sixteen rest camps in the park, and lodging is in traditional African rondavels—round, thatched bungalows with modern facilities and comforts. The guides are trained naturalists who know where to look for the best game.

The safari usually continues to one of the lodges in the private reserves, most likely the beautiful Inyati on the banks of the Sand River. Here guests enjoy a full range of game drives in open land cruisers, and may experience the bush more closely.

One of the benefits of the Sabie-Sand Reserves is that all the owners of this vast tract of land have agreed not to fence their separate properties, so the game wanders freely throughout all its environments. This not only increases the game-viewing opportunities, but is ecologically sound in terms of gene pools, food supply and land use.

The animal populations of the eastern Transvaal are plentiful and stable. Impalas are everywhere; elephants, giraffes, and zebras are common; and lions are almost a certainty in the private reserves where off-road travel is permitted. Hippos and crocodiles inhabit the pools and rivers, and there are herds of wildebeests and Cape buffalo. While not plentiful, there are enough rhinos that one is likely to see one during a stay of two or three days. More elusive, but equally likely to be seen are cheetahs and leopards.

The combination of the vast reaches of Kruger National Park and the more intimate bush experience of the private reserves, coupled with the plenitude of animal life and varied environments, makes this area one of Africa's three top-ranked safari destinations.

"The [lion] cubs gambol and play like kittens; they climb over the adults and tumble about, they spar with each other, they stalk father's black tipped flicking tail and give it a quick bite; when they can find them, they make toys of ostrich eggs and roll them playfully around."

Juliette Huxley: **Wild Lives of Africa,** *1963*

Opposite page: *Lion cubs generally weigh about three pounds (1.4 kg) at birth. They rarely accompany their elders on a hunt until they are at least five months old.*

Pages 116-117: *If you travel to the eastern Transvaal, you'll see plenty of Cape buffalo.*

SAFARI ADVENTURE: NOTES FROM A JOURNAL

THE EASTERN TRANSVAAL:

"In Botswana men die in the bush; here men *live* in the bush." It was late and I sat by a dying camp-fire, sharing a bottle of fine Stellenbosch with Tony Williams, my host in the Rattray Reserve. Not that the bush here had become tamed and no longer wild and free—far from it. Tony referred instead to the happy juxtaposition of primeval African landscape and wildlife with the pleasures and luxuries of civilization.

We arrive at Inyati, after two days exploring Kruger National Park and staying at its rest camps. After miles of travel across open bush-veld, the sand road climbs to a high clearing where wildebeests watch us sadly from a bush airstrip. Inside the Inyati gate is another environment, changed suddenly from the open gray-green veld to the cool, deep greens of a riverine valley, where arching trees shade the thatched cottages from the afternoon sun.

A path leads through a garden and opens out onto a green lawn stretching downward to the white sands and slow-moving waters of the Sand River. Behind the river lies a forest of tall reeds, their long, shining leaves catching glints and sparkles of afternoon sun, their pale plumes turned a froth of silver in the light. Behind this rises a backdrop of bushveld, a slope of green from the valley to the golds of the winter grass and the thorn trees, until these last are silhouetted against the clear, rich blue of the sky. It is the synthesis of the land of which Tony spoke, comfort and civilization set against the stark beauty and harsh realities of the bush.

I could sit right here on the terrace, under the vine of bright orange flowers, and watch the sunset, but I cannot resist an evening game drive.

"I know a place," the ranger tells me, "where we can watch the sun set behind the Drakensburg. We can get there just in time if you don't mind a fast, bumpy ride." We arrive just as the bottom edge of the great round ball touches the rim of the Drakensburg escarpment, lying in low profile against the western horizon. We watch as it slips deeper, at last leaving the whole sky to an orange afterglow that holds every thorn tree in black silhouette against it.

Afterward, with spotlights sweeping the bush, we stalk the animals of the night. Bush hares scamper across the path and a nightjar starts suddenly beside our vehicle. Eyes watch us, glowing green, red, and yellow from the bush around us, the rest hidden in the darkness. We follow a hunting lioness, then lose her in a thick tangle of undergrowth along a deep-cut valley. We are in an open jeep, and when the engine is off, there is nothing to separate us from the night. Night and

Opposite page: *Elephants congregate in separate herds, males in one, females and young in another.*

Below: *The yellow-billed stork fishes for food by walking through the shallow water with its bill open, and snapping it shut when it feels a fish.*

© Gerry Ellis/Ellis Wildlife Collection

day are different worlds in the bush, where night settles swiftly in a blackness like no other. The sounds that fill the air are soft ones—insect chirps, the low song of a Cape turtledove, and the light rustle of the leaves and grass.

At last we go to the wide clearing of the airstrip. The herd of wildebeests is still there, watching us this time, a row of luminous green eyes at the edge of the clearing. The stars are brilliant overhead; each one pierces the blackness and together they trace giant patterns across the sky. There is the Southern Cross and the False Cross, and the long sweep of Scorpio's tail ending just above the trees.

Dinner is in the *boma*, a reed enclosure open to the sky with a campfire in its center. Before the impala steak is served, a trio of dancers moves to the compelling rhythm of African drums. After dinner we gather our chairs closer to the fire and talk long into the night.

Much as I enjoy the game drives, it is during afternoon walks at Inyati that I have learned to appreciate its varied sights, sounds, and smells as well as the colors and textures of its landscapes. Accompanied by two rangers, one armed, we walk along the river to a spot on the bank where a crocodile is sunning. A bateleur swoops from high above us, heads straight for a little francolin, and makes a direct hit. An old giraffe limps slowly to the water hole and stands watching us as little birds pull ticks from his long neck. I recognize the sansevieria, far taller here than in dish gardens in the florist shop, and learn that the bushmen use its fibers to make rope.

From the first afternoon at Mala Mala, the most famous of the Rattray reserves, I understand why people don't refer to staying there. They speak instead of the Mala Mala experience. Like Inyati, it is no ordinary bush camp. Its rondavels are draped in bougainvillea, its lawns lush and green (except

where the warthogs dig, proof that even this posh resort is in the bush). The wide verandas overlook the river across a broad expanse of lawn, and animals graze on the slopes of the opposite side.

But the bush is more at arm's length here. The air of luxury is strong; the rangers serve guests their drinks before dinner, instead of everyone gathering at the bar. A bit more formal, hardly anyone comes to dinner in bush clothes. I try to think of something I want or need before it's offered, but I can't.

The game is all here and in abundance; as elsewhere in these private reserves, first-time guests are astonished at how close we can get to the animals. I have to put on a wide-angle lens to photograph an elephant, we are so close. The rangers here know the game and their habits— each has his favorite pride of lions and recognizes each of the cubs and knows when it was born.

Tonight I want to see a cheetah, so we go cheetah hunting. We search in the dark riverine valleys and at last find a pair. We watch them in the late sun and finally leave them as they disappear into the long shadows. Then we find a kopje from which to watch the sunset. With sundowners comes a little portable *brai* from the back of the car, and soon curried meatballs sizzle over its flame.

In the dark, now, we come upon a herd of Cape buffalo, and we drive into the middle of them. The buffalo stand there, some looking at us, some ignoring us. Two large bulls tussle and one bumps the vehicle with his flank and we appreciate just how big and powerful these animals are. We not only hear them breathing at this distance, we can feel them. From the bush, more pairs of eyes stare at us, glowing in our headlights, disembodied from the rest of the animal like the grin on the Cheshire Cat.

Opposite page: *The cheetah, although among the more elusive animals to spot, hunts later in the morning and earlier in the evening than other big cats, giving the game viewer extra daylight time to see it.*

"There is nothing like one's first, or one's last, camp. Others may be more beautiful, hold more delight and produce greater drama, but those at the beginning and end have a unique quality all their own given them, not by the people who build them, so much as by some abiding symbolism of life."

Laurens van der Post: **The Lost World of the Kalahari,** *1958*

As the sun sets and silhouettes a giant baobab at Mashatu Camp in Botswana, the bush begins to come alive after the heat of the day.

SUPPLIERS AND OUTFITTERS

The following suppliers and agencies can provide information, itineraries, and current rates on safaris to the destinations described in this book:

A World Apart **East Africa**
P. O. Box 44207
Nairobi, Kenya
Fax 254-2-333262
Telex 22526

Classic Tours International **East Africa**
625 North Michigan Avenue **Botswana**
Chicago, Illinois 60611 **(Okavango Delta, Chobe)**
(800) 828-8222

Flamingo Tours of Africa **East Africa**
139A New Bond Street
London W1Y 9FB, England
01-409-2229

Ker Downey Selby **Botswana**
13201 Northwest Freeway **(Chobe, Okavango Delta)**
Houston, Texas 77040
(800) 231-6352

Mountain Travel **East Africa**
6420 Fairmount Avenue
El Cerrito, California 94530
(800) 227-2384

SATOUR **Southern Africa**
747 Third Avenue
New York, New York 10017
(800) TABLE MT

20 Elgin Avenue West,
Suite 1001
Toronto, Ontario MR4 1K8
Canada
(416) 482-7077

Solrep International **Southern Africa**
2524 Nottingham
Houston, Texas 77005
(800) 231-0985

Sporting International **Botswana**
14 Old Bond Street **(Chobe, Okavango Delta)**
London W1X 3DB, England
01-629-2044
Fax 01-491-9177